For Frank
Christmas 67
wi...

CURIOSITIES OF THE SELF

" My life is the s......... of
self realization by the unconscious.
Everything contained within the
unconscious seeks outward manifestati...
and the personality also desires
to evolve out of its unconscious
conditioning factors and to experience
itself as a whole , ————

So it is that I have now
undertaken, in the 53rd year of my
life, to tell my personal myth.
I can only make direct statements
only "tell stories". whether or not
the stories are true is not the
problem. The only question is
whether what I tell is _my_
fable, _my_ truth. .... We are
a psychic process which we do not
control, or only partly direct. Con —
sequently we cannot have any
final judgment about ourselves
or our lives. If we do, we would
know everything "
    " Human life is a dubious experiment "
                    Jung

BOOKS BY THEODOR REIK

Ritual (With a preface by Sigmund Freud)
The Unknown Murderer
Surprise and the Psychoanalyst
From Thirty Years with Freud
Masochism in Modern Man
A Psychologist Looks at Love
Psychology of Sex Relations
Dogma and Compulsion
Listening with the Third Ear
Fragment of a Great Confession
The Secret Self
The Haunting Melody
The Search Within
Creation of Woman
Mystery on the Mountain
The Temptation
Myth and Guilt
Of Love and Lust
The Compulsion to Confess
Sex in Man and Woman
Jewish Wit
The Need to Be Loved
Pagan Rites in Judaism
Voices from the Inaudible
The Unreachables

Illusions we have about ourselves

CURIOSITIES OF THE SELF

THEODOR REIK

The Noonday Press · a division of
Farrar, Straus & Giroux · New York

Author's Note

The three essays presented here originated, independent from each other, during the last years. Although they differ widely in their subject matter, they have certain features in common. All three explore curious or odd phenomena in the life of the individual and of groups—phenomena that rarely, if ever, had been the subjects of psychological or psychoanalytic treatment of many persons. From this point of departure they transcend the area of the individual case and touch general problems.

It was, if I am not mistaken, Jules Lemaître who once remarked that there are always lengths in the confidences of others (*"Il y a toujours des longueurs dans les confidences des autres"*). It must be during those lengths that the trains of thought of the analyst sometimes are led to general problems of the mentioned kind. Those seminal thoughts often re-emerge after many years.

The brief essay on "Time and Tenses" deals with the mental trick all of us contrive to deny death as full annihilation. "Murder in Mind' 'treats the countless cases in which we have unconscious murderous impulses toward those nearest and dearest to us—impulses which arise often from trivial motives. "The Unreachables" tries to trace the destiny of the Jews to their earliest traumatic experiences, showing the repetition-compulsion operating in their vicissitudes, and arrives at utterly unexpected conclusions about the future.

If these three explorations succeed only in making the reader see things in a new light revealing to him startlingly new connections, they will have achieved their purpose.

CONTENTS

THREE / THE UNREACHABLES: *The Repetition Compulsion in Jewish History*

ONE

TIME AND TENSES

Introduction

I feel sleepy, yet I cannot fall asleep, although I had taken two noctettes half an hour ago. There must be something preventing me from sleeping.

The evening I had spent with my friend Otto occurs to me. Otto, an internist, is as old as I am and is also semi-retired. He sees some old patients and is frequently called into consultation by other physicians. His background is quite similar to mine—Viennese-Jewish. He came as I did to the United States, a refugee from Hitler in 1938. We have similar opinions about essential problems of our time.

But yesterday he surprised me with some strange statements. He said, for instance, that neither of us pays enough attention to the question of time. "Don't we read the *New York Times* soon after breakfast and often during it?" I asked. But he did not react to this. Did he perhaps mean it with regard to age? "No," he said. But when we said good-by to each other, he used an old and familiar Viennese saying: "*So jung wer'n me uns auch nimmer sehen*" (Perhaps translatable as "It's a pity we'll never meet again so young.")

I now recall how he began to speak about it. We had just crossed Central Park and he pointed to children playing. "Look at those kids," he said. "All run, whatever else they do. They run in their play and they run on errands. The whole future is before them; why do they hurry? Their greatest wish is perhaps to be grown up. Then when they become adults, they don't run any longer—except in sport, which is a relapse into childhood; they walk. And from then on they become slower and slower. When they grow old, we physicians advise them, 'Slow down!' They should not ascend stairs quickly and they should not even jump up from their chairs. The whole aging process is accompanied by slowing down. The other day I told a very old man not to take a walk, but to crawl a walk. That slowing down continues until they are unable to move quickly and ends in that state of immovability we call rigor mortis."

I had listened attentively to his building a bridge between movement and age. Of course, I could not deny the truth of what he said, but I asked: "What do you want to prove?" "Nothing," he said ill-humoredly.

I am now, however, too sleepy to pursue his train of thought, and I forgot about it until it came to mind on a long detour. At a certain point of my psychoanalytic work I had suddenly to struggle with the problem of time, or rather with the disconcertingly problematical nature of time. My thoughts had almost nothing to do with Einstein's theory of the relativity of time, whose problems they only touched once, tangentially. They took their point of departure from an early clinical case in my psychoanalytic practice. From there the question arises: What does time mean to you and to me?

The Past

We start, of course, with the past since there seems no possible doubt about the past, whose facts are changeless, firm and fixed. Aristotle said that not even God can change the past.

Since we are especially interested in the meaning of the past, we will explore not so much the external data and the facts themselves, but their significance for the individual and for groups.

The researchers who have not only the best opportunities but also the necessary means and the urgent motives to revivify the past of individuals are the psychoanalysts. They explore the inner experiences of their patients and also their own.

However, psychoanalysis is not a courtroom procedure. We don't expect patients to tell us the truth, the whole truth, and nothing but the truth. We are not even especially interested in all the events of their past life; rather, we want to know how events have affected them emotionally.

To revive the past for them is an essential part of our task. In this reconstruction of the past we learn its meaning for the patient, its emotional significance.

Let us assume a three-year-old boy or girl witnessed a spat between his parents. In his memory it was a catastrophic event, filling him with panic. In reality it was perhaps not more than an everyday scene in which father and mother had words.

We find it difficult to imagine the terror a little boy felt when he lost the ticket the Chinese laundryman had given him, and it is hard to feel what he experienced in not daring to go home without it. He was sure that he had committed a crime.

Childhood memories, recalled during puberty, are often distorted and transformed. In psychoanalytic sessions, such reports are mostly a concoction of fact and fiction. It is the past as it reflects itself in the patients' minds.

Later memories also, as they appear in flares and flashes, are influenced by various unconscious factors. The patients sometimes confuse the time of events, deceive themselves not only about the facts, but also their own emotional and mental processes. They often omit certain thoughts and feelings, and even oftener are mistaken about their character in interpreting earlier experiences. And just as patients frequently deceive themselves about facts, they also deceive themselves about emotions and mental processes connected with facts. They see a crime where there is none, and feel innocent where they unconsciously felt guilty. They often see victory where there is actually defeat, vice versa. They state that they loved, where they loved and hated at the same time, and they assert that they felt repelled where they unconsciously were attracted. The analyst listening to them (also "with the third ear") must correct their mistakes in fact and fiction, but he himself is sometimes mistaken in the reconstruction of the truth.

He sometimes gets the impression that the patients have become legendary figures to themselves. The whole problematic nature of the past becomes clear only when it is seen through the eyes of a skeptical explorer.

I said before that one of the essential tasks of the psychoanalyst is to revivify the past, but this is by no means always possible and is often not even desirable.

Here is one instance of this kind: A patient in her late thirties has many complaints about her husband, for instance that he sometimes had to make business trips lasting two or three days, that he earns too little money so that her wealthy father must make monthly contributions to the household, and so on.

These complaints, which I had at first taken seriously, appeared later on to be a cover for feelings of a very different kind. The change in my concept of her case did come about in a strange way. At a certain point of her psychoanalytic treatment I encouraged her to overcome her resistances and to tell me all the critical and hostile thoughts she had not expressed concerning me. By and by she did so, but it was accompanied by very vivid feelings of hate toward me. This emotional reaction was paradoxical; most patients feel freer and better when they have had an opportunity to express their criticism and hostile feelings.

It was not difficult to guess what was the chief motive for her paradoxical behavior. She was so convinced that I would feel angry and disgusted with her—that I would consider her, as she said, a "horrible bitch"—so that she hated me whenever she said something in criticism. Her hate was thus a projection of what she imagined I would feel toward her, namely, that she was a detestable and hateful person. As if by a powerful searchlight, the case was illuminated by an understanding of her attitude toward me. (She had never expressed her complaints to her husband because she was afraid he would hate and condemn her.)

The patient had been a very naughty child at home as well as in school. She was unruly and was often scolded and punished. Her father once threatened to send her to a reform school. Her disobedient and rebellious behavior as a child was especially caused by the serious conflict between her father and her mother and which almost led to their divorce.

This rebellious attitude continued also when she went to college and, later, when she became almost promiscuous.

She then fell in love with her present husband and has since become an exemplary wife and mother. But what of the complaints about her husband, uttered at the same time as she said what a wonderful man he was? It is transparent that other concealed, unconscious motives are operating here, since it became obvious that the complaints had no serious foundations.

It was true that her husband sometimes had to go on a business trip for a few days, but other men in the same profession were away from home much oftener and for a longer period. The considerable amount her father contributed to the household was given voluntarily and with great satisfaction. The patient had a beautiful house in the suburbs of New York, had an excellent housekeeper and helper for the children, she had cars, and all sorts of conveniences.

There remained only one reason for her discontent: It was unconscious guilt feeling, or, better still, the feeling of, "I don't deserve such a good husband, such lovely children, and such a luxurious life after what I have done in my youth." This feeling of unworthiness was, of course, the unconscious expression of her own inferiority attitude, which she became aware of only during the psychoanalytic treatment.

But let us return to our problem. We discussed the individual past as it is reflected not only in the minds of our neurotic patients, but also in the minds of so-called "normal" people. The reports they can give us are full of distortions, displacements, disavowals, and other unconscious processes, to such an extent that an objective picture of the individual past is almost unobtainable. The past is in reality full of mysteries. Even when some are clarified, enough remain to blur the picture of the past.

The Relativity of Time

We said that to revive and to reconstruct the past is one of the essential tasks of the analyst, who cannot understand the emotional situation of the patient without this preliminary work. The analyst who would think with Shakespeare, "What's past, is prologue," has to explore and recapture the past because it determined the actual situation of the patient.

Yet there are cases in which the analyst cannot fulfill this necessary work. What follows is an instance of this kind. When I was a young psychoanalyst, Freud once referred to me the case of a professor of medicine. He was an older man, at least twenty years my senior. Freud must have had a special reason for not referring this man to a physician. Discretion forbids me to enter into their discussion (although the man died many years ago), but one reason can easily be guessed. Freud perhaps did not want this professor of medicine to be treated by one of the Viennese physicians. The doctor was famous in his medical specialty and saw many patients from all over Europe.

His chief complaint was the following: Whenever he had to examine a woman, he had an erection. That had never happened to him during his many years of practice, but had for several months become an everyday experience. Physicians at that time wore a kind of cutaway (in Vienna called a *Salonrock*) and it was a source of great embarrassment to the doctor that the erection was noticeable to the women he examined.

We started the psychoanalytic treatment and he spoke of his family, his parents, and often of his brother Julius, who was much younger than he and towards whom he had a remote relationship for a long time.

While he was complaining about the embarrassing symptom of the erection in his practice, his relationship to me changed in a surprising manner. He had always been polite and ready to listen to me, but now, entering my consultation room almost daily, he showed a strange behavior. He brought me gifts each time he came; first a pack of cigarettes of the brand I preferred, the next time bonbons of a special kind, then a box of pâté de foie gras, and finally flowers. I asked him not to do this and finally forbade it, but he cleverly hid the presents and left them behind in my room.

There was no doubt what this behavior meant; it was an expression of his strong positive transference. It could not have been accidental that he mentioned his younger brother. Under the cover of his heterosexual overexcitement, his earlier homosexual tendencies came to the surface.

In my predicament I asked Freud's advice. He listened attentively to my report and then said: "It is better to break off the analytic treatment now and send the patient to Professor Eppinger." Professor Eppinger was the specialist in hormone treatment at the Vienna University.

Freud reminded me of Thomas Mann's story "Death in Venice," published a few years before, and of other cases in which such a change appeared in mature years. The treatment by Professor Eppinger was not only indicated by reasons of expediency, but also with regard to the time at our disposal. The patient was approaching his sixties and his psychoanalysis would have taken several years.

It was, so to speak, a poor investment in time, whereas the hormone treatment would require only a few months. As I was told later, that treatment proved very successful.

I mention this case not only because psychoanalysis was, so to speak, contraindicated, but because the moment of the relativity of time had a great part in the problem. It was this case mentioned before, which awakened that train of thought concerning the problematic character of time.

I have here exhaustively discussed this character in the life of individuals, but how is it with the history of collectives, of groups and nations? Are the facts of the past at least here firm and unchangeable? Samuel Butler once remarked: "It has been said that although God cannot alter the past, historians can." [1] They do.

Take the history most familiar to us all. We still do not know whether figures such as Abraham and Isaac are historical persons or if their stories merely reflect tribal movements. It is misleading to assume that archaeology proves the truth of the Bible. [2] It proves at most that the description of patriarchal life corresponded to reality. [3] Harold H. Rowley recently asserted that none of the patriarchs is mentioned outside the Scriptures, and no incident in which "they figured is recorded in any contemporary source." [4] So much for the biblical stories; they were transformed and distorted, like the life stories of individuals to whom we are listening.

How about past events in the life of nations? Have we not documents and inscriptions and other indications of the past? They leave no doubt about the historicity of early events. There is apparently no place for skepticism. But even when we can read them, they are full of mythological allusion and are often written or edited many years after the events. The prehistory and early history of people are forever clouded.

Let us imagine a scholar who is devoted to study and dedicated to the writing of a people's history, let us say of the French nation. Anatole France gives us a good picture of such a historian whose life was centered on one goal: to write the story of a nation. No difficulty could deter him. He went to archaeologists and palaeographers of his own country and of others. They looked at him with contempt and seemed to say: "Do we write history? Do we try to get the truth out of a text, a document? Not at all. We just print the text. He who writes history must be very vain and takes pleasure in invention."

Discouraged, the historian turned to a member of the Academy and asked his advice. But this clever old man merely shrugged and asked, "Why do you want to write a history if it is only customary to copy the known ones? If you had an original idea or opinion and presented men and things in an unexpected light, you would only surprise your reader. The reader does not like to be surprised. In a historical work he searches for something he already knows. The historians copy each. Do as they do and avoid the appearance of priggishness!"

We have been discussing the past so circumstantially because at first sight it seems unchangeable. We recognize then that this is not so, that the past is subject to transformations and changes, like everything else under the sun.

The Present

Sobered by this result, we turn to the present. Here, at least, we feel we are on firm ground. The past pales to insignificance compared with the vividness of the present. It is as if the moment that we can grasp is the substance and the past just a shadow. The present is reality, immediacy, solidity.

It tickles the intellect when we take the present, the now and here, under our psychological microscope. The present cannot be compared with any other time. Don't we say, "There is no time like the present"? Don't we feel that the present is our precious possession, and are we not admonished to enjoy the moment?

Such enthusiastic praise and glorification of the present should make us cautious. Are we not sometimes deceived by a Fata Morgana? Doesn't such a mirage appear more real than its actual surroundings to the thirsty, tired traveler?

What is the present? A child has a balloon in his hands; in the next split second the balloon freely sails in the air. You want to cross a street, and just as you take your first step, the traffic sign changes: "Don't walk!" You admire the face or the figure of a woman, and in the next minute you see blemishes in it. Such an intercurrent impression sometimes stops you in mid-sentence.

Is it necessary to point out that the same character is valid for the life of collectives? While the President of the United States or the Secretary of State speaks of the present crisis in Vietnam or on Cyprus, the whole situation is perhaps changed by an unexpected incident. The crisis continues, of course, because crises last long, but what those statesmen say about the "present crisis" is no longer true. Some shots have changed the "present crisis" into a past one within a split second. You discuss the present situation on the stock market, but while you speak the ticker shows it has changed in the middle of your sentence. What you have said is already part of the past.

What is the result of such an exploration of the present? It vanishes before our eyes or, rather, it gets lost. It would amount to an overstatement to describe the present as short-lived. It would be as if you were to say a baby who died at the moment of birth, as so many babies do, was short-lived.

There is only the past and the future. The present marks only the split second of transition from one tense to the other. Yes, we suspect that there is no such a thing as present, and that it was constructed by the grammarians who needed a temporary bridge between the past and the future. Those of us who are initiated into the secret psychology of the tenses, know that there is no present, because in the moment you think of it or speak about it, it already belongs to the past, along with events a thousand years ago.

The Future

Our exploration arrived at the most uncertain time of all: the future—which we do not know anything about. From territories that we considered firm and permanent we came to an area that is considered dubious and which we cannot anticipate. There is no guide to lead us.

This part should really be introduced by the report of a conversation I had with a physician in Lake Placid, New York. I sometimes drove to the town with this doctor and we discussed various things during the drive. Once I expressed the opinion that people who are ill sometimes become accustomed after a while to their disease and adapt themselves accordingly. The physician, a medical director of the Lake Placid Memorial Hospital, argued. He sketched the case history of a middle-aged patient who a week before had demanded: "And am I supposed to carry this terrible symptom with me for the rest of my life?" The doctor soberly added: "The rest of his life lasted two and a half days." Well, that's an unfortunate case, but what I want to say is that we cannot see into the future which is doubtful. Can we know whether a coronary attack will not kill us in the next minute or a car run us over? On the other hand, we do not know what piece of luck we may have the next minute. The uncertainty of the future is for us no longer a symbolic expression but a cliché. No crystal ball we can look into, no fortune teller who predicts it, nor any other means can remove that uncertainty.

Compared with the other times, the future is characterized by uncertainty. We are kept in suspense or left in the dark about what awaits us there. René Descartes said: *"Cogito, ergo sum"* (I think, therefore I am).[5] But this sentence is, of course, incorrect. There can be awareness of living without thinking. Also, other criteria of living might be uncertain. Yet past and present show that we were or are alive. Is anything as undoubted or beyond all doubt imaginable for the future? Yes; in this sea of uncertainty there is one single fact that is absolutely and undeniably certain: We must die.

Our Relationship to Death

In 1961 a strange book was published, *In the Midst of Life*.[6] The writer was Thomas Bell, who faced the prospect of certain death in six months and who died a few weeks after he completed his book.

A few sentences from it are enough to show that the certainty of death in so short a time appeared to the patient often as unreal. The thought occurred to him: "This can't happen to me. Such things happen only to other people. Me with a malignant tumor?" He considered it nonsense that he had only a few months to live. It remained unreal.

Yet the thought of his death follows him. The kitchen calendar shows him the whole year at a glance. He often lets his eyes run over it. January to December and back again, and he wonders which of those days on it will be his last.

In a paper, first published in 1915, Freud [7] clearly showed us that our attitude to death is unconsciously quite similar to that of this patient. We are, of course, ready to maintain that we shall die, but in psychological reality we behave as if we refuse to believe it. Our own death is unimaginable, and whenever we attempt to imagine it we realize that we are surviving as spectators. Unconsciously we are convinced that we shall not die; that we are immortal.

We have thus a divided attitude to our death: a conventional one and an unconscious one in which we cannot conceive of ourselves as being dead. Everybody knows that the religions came to compromise solutions, as to a life beyond, to a kind of shadow life, and so on. Ghosts and demons were invented; paradise and hell. The essence of all those fairy tales for grownups is that the fact of death is not denied, only its significance as complete annihilation. Freud stated that our conscience is inaccessible to the idea of death and we do not possess any instinct that prepares us for the belief in our own death.

Freud tells us that we live psychologically beyond our means in denying the truth and we had better give death the place in actuality and in our thoughts which properly belongs to it. It is an admonition as valuable as any other. To relinquish or to discard such an illusion to which we unconsciously adhere is difficult. How can this be done?

The Suspension of Disbelief

When the poets Coleridge and Wordsworth were together, they often discussed literary themes. They agreed that Coleridge's endeavor should be directed to persons and characters supernatural, or at least romantic. Yet from our inward nature a human interest and "a semblance of truth sufficient to procure for these shadows of imagination that willing suspension of disbelief for the moment which constitutes poetic faith."

These conversations between the two poets are communicated in the fourteen chapters of Coleridge's *Biographica*

Literaria, wherein he adds that with this view in mind he wrote "The Ancient Mariner" and other poems.[8]

What interests us in our context is the felicitous phrase "a willing suspension of disbelief." Do we not undergo such an actual suspension when we for instance attend a performance of *Hamlet*? We do not believe in ghosts. Yet we suspend our disbelief when we accept the old king's ghost and as we listen to his words.

I do not hesitate to transfer that superbly felicitous phrase to the area of our two contrasting attitudes toward death. If we could be honest with ourselves, we would imagine that our death is an event that ends all. That means that when we are dead we are as inorganic as that chair or that table, and soon not more than a small heap of ashes. Our death ends all.

And now look at our eighty-year-old men and women! They behave as if they believed themselves immortal. They are interested in the future of space flight, in the attempts to reach the moon, in the consequences of the population explosion, in events of a future which they can never share. We do not even discuss their worries about their grandchildren nor of their thoughts of how to provide for the distant future of their own children.

If a crudely realistic view of their death would be accepted, they would certainly not do this. Is a chair interested in the destiny of those children, or a table in the future of space flight? [9] In a short time they will be as lifeless and inorganic as those objects, which do not have such interests.

Isn't a dying man a man without a future? He is indifferent to it, whether after him comes the deluge or paradise.

At this point, I return to Coleridge's phrase of the "willing suspension of disbelief." Here, in denying one's total annihilation, is a suspension of disbelief, much more grandiose than the one operating in poetic works, let us say in *Hamlet.*

I consider it possible that a future psychiatric commentator on Shakspeare's play would declare all the scenes with Hamlet's father were nothing but fantasies or, better still, thoughts of the son, who oscillates between suspicions of his mother and uncle and doubt about them. This means that all those scenes with the old king are projections of the prince's thoughts. He borrows words and sentences from his father, phrases of suspicions aroused long ago and now emerging as hallucinations. The prince would thus be a paranoiac, but all actions of the play would follow as now.

I said the "willing suspension of disbelief" in the case of our death must be much more radical and deep-reaching. Which means, in other words, unconsciously we really think we are surviving our death in some form or other. In some form—that could also mean in the memory of our children and grandchildren, of our friends and relatives who continue to live and who remember us—rarely or often. Otherwise how could we, so to speak, live with those we leave behind?

When we provide for their lives, when we are interested in the future of our community or of our nation, it can be only because we willingly suspended our disbelief that our death means complete annihilation and because we cannot imagine that we shall be dust. Yet the Bible declares, "For dust thou art, and unto dust shalt thou return." (Genesis 3:19.)

Only that wonderful "willing suspension of disbelief" enables us to look hopefully into the future of our children and of mankind.

TWO

MURDER IN MIND

"This Essay, such as it is, was thought by some who know of it, not amiss to be published; that so many things, remarkable, dis-per'd before, now brought under one view, might not hazard to be otherwise lost, nor the labor lost of collecting them"

John Milton
A Brief History of Muscovia (1682)

Who Wrote It?

Freud, who had—I don't know why—an astonishing trust in my being well read, frequently asked me to find this or that quotation which occurred to him from time to time. As far as I can remember, I failed him only once. Thereby hangs a tale.

Freud had asked me in May, 1929, where in Rousseau's works the story of the murder of a mandarin was to be found. One of Freud's letters to me, published in my book *The Search Within*,[1] reminds me of that search.

> *Tegel, October 20, 1929*
> *Dear Herr Doctor:*
> *The famous story of the mandarin* (tuer son mandarin) *comes from Rousseau after all. Could you tell me without going to too much trouble where it is to be found?*
>
> *Cordially yours,*
> *Freud*

I must have written Freud that I could not find the story in Rousseau's works, in spite of my diligent search. I had hunted for it in the writings of Rousseau, whose style I admired, but whom I did not like. (Much later I read that Anatole France also intensely disliked that Genevese writer whom he called a *"pis-froid,"* a man without temperament or without moral courage.)

Freud perhaps thought that the passage was familiar to me because he knew that I had studied French literature, although psychology had been my major at the University of Vienna. He had also read my Ph.D. thesis on Flaubert and his *Temptation of St. Anthony*[2] which applied the methods of depth psychology to the problem of artistic creation.

The phrase *"tuer son mandarin"* I had first heard many years before, in Paris, in 1911. I still remember the occasion. Someone had spoken of an office clerk whose employer was old and whose position the younger man hoped to inherit. I remember that I had later looked up the expression in *Larousse*. I found the phrase *"le bouton du mandarin"* and *"le paradoxe du mandarin"* besides *"tuer le mandarin."* *Larousse* calls it a "literary allusion" and explains it in the following manner. "If it would be sufficient, in order to inherit from a very rich man whom one had never seen and with whom one had never spoken (for instance a mandarin in faraway China), to push a button that would kill him, who would hesitate to push that button?"

The second time I came upon that phrase was in a paper by Freud, in the magazine *Imago* published early in 1913.[3] In this paper Freud discusses our attitude toward death, one's own and that of others.

Freud states that if we are judged according to our unconscious wishes we are, like the primal men, a gang of murderers. He knows, of course, that such statements will be rejected as libels and therefore points to thinkers who could not have been influenced by psychoanalysis. Many of them believe that we are unconsciously ready to pay no regard to the prohibition of murder and Freud quotes a single famous example. "In *Le Père Goriot* Balzac alludes to a passage in the works of J. J. Rousseau where that author asks the reader what he would do if, without leaving Paris and, of course, without being discovered, he could kill, with great profit to himself, an old mandarin in Peking by a mere act of will. Rousseau implies that he would not give much for the life of that dignitary. *'Tuer son mandarin'* has become a proverbial phrase for this secret readiness present even in modern man."

That passage in *Le Père Goriot* appears important enough to quote it. Young Eugene de Rastignac has a conversation with his friend, the medical student Bianchon:[4]

> *"I'm tortured by evil thoughts."*
> *"What kind of thoughts? You can cure thoughts."*
> *"How do you do it?"*
> *"By giving in to them."*
> *"You may laugh; you don't know what it's all about.
> Have you read Rousseau?"*
> *"Yes."*
> *"Do you remember that passage in which he asks the
> reader what he would do if he could become
> wealthy by killing an old Chinese mandarin, with-
> out leaving Paris, just by an act of will?"*
> *"Yes."*
> *"Well then?"*
> *"Oh, I'm on my thirty-third mandarin."*
> *"Don't joke about it. Come, if it were proved to you that
> the thing was possible and that all you'd need to
> do would be to nod your head, would you do it?"*
> *"Is your mandarin very old? Oh, well, young or old,
> healthy or paralytic, good Lord. . . . Oh, the
> devil! Well, no."*
> *"You're a decent fellow, Bianchon. But suppose that you
> love a woman enough to sell your soul for her,
> and she needs money, a lot of money for her
> clothes, for her carriage, in short, for all her no-
> tions?"*

> *"But you're taking my reason away from me, and you want me to use it."*

At this point we are confronted with a multitude of questions, of a literary and psychological kind. To mention only a few: since Freud had attributed the paradox of the mandarin to J. J. Rousseau in 1915, what made him wish to locate the passage in 1929? Did he himself doubt that Rousseau was its author? Why did I not find the passage in Rousseau's works?

Let us first discuss the literary problem. I said before that I could not find that passage in Rousseau's works. Let me now add that no one found it. Some old dictionary of quotations perhaps still attributes the passage to *Emile* by Rousseau, but it is not there. Let me quote some new authors about that misquotation. P. Dupré in his new *Encyclopedia of Quotations*[5] says that one generally has, relying on Balzac (*"sure la foi de Balzac"*) attributed the *"paternité de ce mot"* to Rousseau, but it is a mistake. It is more likely that the real author was Chateaubriand. Another work by O. Guerlac also states[6] that nobody until now has been able to discover this discussion of a case of conscience in the works of the Genevese philosopher. Guerlac assumes that Balzac believed that he had read the passage in Rousseau, although it is more probable that he took the formula from Chateaubriand's *Le Génie du Christianisme*.[7]

In a chapter on remorse and conscience, that famous author asks: "If you could by a simple wish kill a man in China and inherit his fortune in Europe. . . would you be willing to carry out this desire?"

Guerlac assumes that Balzac had added the word "mandarin."

A literary historian, Paul Ronai,[8] has indicated an earlier work of Balzac, a novel called *Annette et le criminel*, published under a pseudonym in 1824, ten years before *Le Père Goriot*. In this novel an abbé asks a similar question in a sermon. The priest addresses his audience directly: "You, down there, if you could by a single glance kill a man in New Holland and no one on earth would know it, and you could by this semi-crime obtain a great fortune. . . ." and so on. Here New Holland takes the place of China.

It is thus likely that Balzac was the victim of a trick of memory and that Chateaubriand was the originator of the problem.

Let us put aside the literary problem for the time being and turn our attention to the first psychological question that interests us. After Freud had quoted Balzac's allusion to Rousseau, what made him turn again to that "famous story of the mandarin" fourteen years later?

Since I could not find the passage in Rousseau's works, Freud mentioned the story only in a footnote of his book *Civilization and Its Discontents*,[9] whose first draft was finished in 1929 and sent to the printer in November of that year. Before we turn to that psychological problem, let us try to answer a preliminary question: What made Freud trust Balzac's statement that the passage was to be found in the works of Rousseau, in spite of the fruitlessness of my prolonged and patient search? Truthfully, we don't know. It is perhaps permissible to point out that Freud had a personal attitude toward the works of Honoré de Balzac. We know, for instance, that Freud as a very young man warned his younger sister Anna not to read Balzac because it would have a bad influence on her.[10] We know that the last book he read was Balzac's *La Peau de Chagrin*.[11] We are unable to go beyond that point and return to our original question.

In order to find an answer, we must first consider in which context Freud treats that problem allegedly first posed by Rousseau. We feel that it will be dealt with in a different connection from that of fourteen years before. Freud points out that evil, to the child, originally is that for which one is punished by the parents with loss of their love. At this phase of development guilt feeling is obviously anxiety concerning the impending loss of parental love. It cannot be anything else with small children. But also with many adults little is changed when the place of the father or of both parents is taken by the community or society. Therefore they permit themselves the evil that promises pleasure, if they are certain that the authorities will not know anything about it or cannot act against them. The anxiety of many adults is thus directed only to the discovery of their misdeeds. It is at this point that Freud says in a footnote, "Think of Rousseau's famous mandarin." [12]

So much for the context in which that mandarin story reappears. But we must also consider the difference in the psychological situation of the man Freud in 1915 and in 1929. We do not think only of the psychological difference between a man who is fifty-nine years old and the same man when he is seventy-three. In this particular case I think especially of the different situation between a healthy man and the same man whose life is threatened by a dangerous disease.

We know that Freud had cancer, which was detected in September, 1923.[13] In 1929 he was in Berlin with Professor Schroeder, who prepared a new prosthesis for him. At the time he wrote to me from Tegel, he was staying at the sanatorium, being treated by Professor Schroeder.

Does the psychological situation, in which Freud knew that he was afflicted with cancer of the throat, cast light on the fact that he thought again of the problem of killing the mandarin? That situation made it, of course, necessary to face the possibility of his own death, made him perhaps think of the death of his father, the wool merchant Jacob

Freud, who had died at the age of eighty-one, and of his mother who lived even longer. Freud himself was seventy-two or seventy-three when he wrote *Civilization and Its Discontents*. As a matter of fact, he died ten years later.

Besides the natural turn of his thoughts in the direction of death we cannot see any reason why he should have thought of Rousseau's famous mandarin. There is, it seems, no way leading from his psychology at this age to the re-emergence of that idea of the murder of the mandarin. There must be a way, perhaps a detour, to the heart of the problem. It cannot be that here is the beginning of the end. It is perhaps the end of the beginning.

Here is the subject of literary detective work, similar though much less important than who wrote Shakespeare's plays.

At all events, we turned easily from literary detective work to the area of psychological detective work. We took the case of the student and the mandarin for granted, but should it not be re-examined? Are such murderous wishes experienced only by a crackpot minority, and are they alien to us normal people? Or do such fantasies form an undercurrent in everyone's life?

Thirty-Five Years Later

Since our way is blocked, we have time to turn to some questions still unanswered; yes, even to a question not yet mentioned. There is, for instance, a personal one. What made me return to this subject after thirty-five years? My search for a passage in Rousseau was broken off in 1929. I considered it then the failure of a mission. It is now May, 1964.

Various impressions, some doubtlessly remaining unconscious, must have combined in bringing about this regression to an abandoned literary puzzle. (Is it only a literary one, I ask myself?) The first thought association occurring to me is Freud's article "Dostoevsky and Parricide." [15] Why just this paper? It must be that it was published in the fall of 1928, immediately preceding *Civilization and Its Discontents.* But there are other reasons for the emergence of that thought association. For instance, that I wrote a critical essay on that Dostoevsky paper and that Freud replied in a long letter, that main part of which I published with his permission. That letter is dated April 14, 1929.[16] There are certainly other reasons for that thought association, not yet accessible to me.[17]

In pursuit of my thought associations, I began rereading the Dostoevsky study (I had not read it for many years). To my astonishment this reading elicits a new comment. It is perhaps inconsequential, but it is spontaneous and cannot be brushed aside.

In this essay, Freud comments that it cannot be accidental that the three literary masterworks of all time deal with the same subject, namely, with the murder of the father: the *King Oedipus* of Sophocles, Shakespeare's *Hamlet,* and Dostoevsky's *Brother Karamazov.* He then discusses the different ways in which the Greek drama, the Shakespeare play, and the Russian novel treat and disguise the crime of parricide. He deals with Dostoevsky at full length, stating that the unconscious temptation of parricide decided the choice of the subject in *The Brothers Karamazov.*

At this point I interrupt my reading and listen (with the

third ear) to the critical thoughts emerging in me. I wondered why Freud had not remarked that these three literary masterworks have another important common feature. The crime and the criminal are not known from the very beginning. They have to be discovered, to be found out. In other words, here are mystery stories in the form of two plays and a novel. The hero is the detective and the criminal in one person. Oedipus is determined to find the truth about himself. He says:

> *My mind abideth strongly*
> *To know the roots, how, low so ere they be*
> *Which grew to Oedipus.*

How can he, he asks, "refrain from knowing all"? Ten or twelve years after the crime a pestilence has fallen on Thebes and this becomes the divine sign for it, that the criminal must be discovered.

The detective Hamlet has to convince himself of the crime and the criminal by means of that play within the play, by tricking and trapping the killer. For nearly four hundred years Hamlet speaks to us with a voice most like the voice of Shakespeare.

In *The Brothers Karamazov*, there is, it is true, a legal procedure; but, as Freud remarked, this is not important itself. It is inconsequential, says Freud, "who really committed the crime, but as far as psychology is concerned, the question is, who willed it and when it was committed, welcomed it. Except Alyosha, all three brothers are equally guilty."

The next thought association returned, strangely enough, to the already mentioned article of Paul Ronai[18] concerning the phrase *"tuer son mandarin."* This literary historian points out that the figure of the criminal Vautrin and of his hypnotic will-power in Balzac's *Père Goriot* is still neglected by critics. "Here is no longer a man, but the example of a degenerate nation," says a critic. Vautrin's conviction that his own will is absolute law, conferred upon him, makes him come close to a figure of Dostoevsky, namely, to Raskolnikov.

Raskolnikov believes that certain exceptional men have the right to kill. Those men of genius might commit murder in the interest of their success and would kill men as if they were insects. He divides mankind into ordinary and extraordinary men. The latter, the Mahomets and Napoleons, must by their very nature, their superiority, be criminals. Raskolnikov considers himself such a superman and thus explains his murder of the old woman Ivanova.

Is it not apparent that Freud never mentions Raskolnikov nor *Crime and Punishment*? He does not speak of them, neither in the essay on Dostoevsky, nor in the study "Some Character Types Met with in Psychological Work." [19] He does not even mention Raskolnikov when he speaks of exceptions, of types who consider themselves so exceptional that they think everything forbidden to others is permissible to them. Also he doesn't speak of Vautrin in Balzac's *Père Goriot*. It is a most eloquent silence that Freud keeps.

The following thought association surprised me because it concerned a detective or mystery story I read a few weeks ago. Since I have become old, I have increasingly lost the taste for the average kind of fiction. Love, hate, and the meetings and meltings of couples, their conflicts and reconciliations, no longer interest me very much. Along with the literature of my own scientific area, I read detective stories. Before falling asleep I like to read a few pages especially of Georges Simenon and to follow the deductions of his Inspector Maigret (in French, if possible).

Since a Maigret mystery was not available at the public

library that day, I took another new book whose title attracted me: *The Evil Wish*, by Jean Potts.[20] I opened the book, and on the second page read the following quotation from Hesiod. "The evil wish is most evil to the wisher." Well, that's not a bad insight for an old Greek who lived eight hundred years before Christ. I read the book.

I had often wondered before why the evil or murderous wish had been neglected in most descriptions of great criminals. Most murders are not only "premeditated," but also "pre-imagined." Except those murders committed on the spur of the moment, except those which the French call "*crimes passionels*," the deeds are pre-acted in fantasy. Here, it seems, was such an example.

The plot is soon told. Two grown-up girls, Lucy and Maria Knapp, live with their father, a widowed physician. The doctor has an affair with his pretty nurse and plans to marry her, which would mean that the girls would lose their home. They find this out by eavesdropping on the couple's conversation on a certain occasion. The sisters carefully plan to poison the father. Before they can carry out the plot, the physician and the nurse are killed in a car accident. Maria and Lucy have a "left-over murder" and "are guilty of murder" without having murdered anybody.

There are a few good observations and insights in this study of guilt; for instance, when one of the sisters suddenly experiences longings for the father whom she wanted to murder. However, the latter part of the story peters out.

It also occurs to me now how I arrived from thinking of *The Brothers Karamazov* to this mystery story. I must have wondered whether the women—in this case two sisters—would have been able to kill the father. I now remember also a fleeting thought reminding me of Lady Macbeth who says of the king,[21]

> *Had he not resembled*
> *My father as he slept, I had done 't.*

The next thought association concerns my last patient (the last person I treated before I broke off psychoanalytic practice after having reached the age of seventy-five). He was an intelligent lawyer with various neurotic complaints. He had improved considerably during the psychoanalytic treatment, but at a certain point I encountered an amazingly strong resistance. The most important neurotic symptoms would not yield. Obviously he had put me in the place of his father, who had died when the patient was seventeen and with whom he had had many conflicts. He had developed a positive transference to me and understood his emotional difficulties well without, however, the energy or the will to change them.

During one of his psychoanalytic sessions he surprised me with the following declaration: "Yesterday it occurred to me that I really did not want to give you the satisfaction of being completely cured. I thought I would rather wait until you were dead." Here again we run into the wish of father's death (or rather of a father-representative figure) in connection with a defiant attitude.

I was tempted to assure him that he would not have long to wait, but of course I said nothing. Finally we conquered even this last stubborn resistance and his symptoms receded and disappeared.

Looking back at the sequence of my thought associations, I wondered: I started from a literary puzzle, namely, from the authorship of that phrase *"tuer son mandarin"* and wound up with mystery stories.

How did I arrive from a who-wrote-it to a whodunit? Here surely was the entrance into that secret compartment I was searching for.

I was tired of the fruitless pursuit of my thought associations. I was closing my eyes. Suddenly an amazing idea emerged from my vague images.

At first I had the utmost difficulty getting hold of that thought. It hovered and fluttered about like a butterfly. Whenever I thought I had it, it had flown beyond reach, and then when I had given up, it was suddenly quite near.

The thought then almost pounced upon me while it mystified me. When I extricated myself from the bewilderment, I was able to envisage and formulate the idea.

It concerns that problem of the mandarin: the assumption in Balzac's version as well as that of Chateaubriand is that the young man is in Paris, that the Chinese dignitary is in Peking. They never knew each other, have never seen each other.

This is where my new idea takes over: Disregard for a moment the geographical distance (it is a far cry from Paris to Peking) and the racial differences; what remains? Here is a young man with no money and an old man with plenty of it and whose fortune the young man will inherit. If you concede that change for the sake of argument, what prevents you from taking another step in the same direction? The result: There is a son who wishes the father dead in order to get his money.

What we need is not fiction, but psychological fact. Money has certainly a strange and powerful effect on human behavior. Money is a compelling motive for murder in imagination, but it is by no means the only and the dominant incentive. We know, for instance, the power of sexual envy and jealousy. There are also thought murders in the war between sexes. As a matter of psychological fact, more murders in imagination are performed than in the war between nations which are distinguished by material massacres. To give a single example: A young woman whom I treated in

Vienna often felt very angry with her boy friend. It became clear in analytic sessions that he left her sexually unsatisfied. Once when she had been left high and dry in sexual intercourse, she caught herself horrified in the fantasy that she would castrate and kill the young man. She ended the affair shortly afterward.

We know how intense the wishes originating in the Oedipus situation affect young men and even men not so young. We also know the inevitability of such unconscious murderous thoughts: Every man must once unconsciously step over the body of his father.

A student of mine, Dr. Arthur Jones, reminded me later of some lines from the preface to the last volume of *Jean Christophe* by Romain Rolland. The writer says that he had described the tragedy of his generation which was nearing its end, and continues; "You young men of today, march over us, trample us under your feet and press onward. Be ye greater and happier than we." (Dated by Romain Rolland October, 1912.)

The idea that had occurred to me perhaps solved the *"le problème du mandarin"* but it left the question why Freud came back to that phrase again (as far as I know, it is the only example of repeating a quotation, and a misquotation at that, in Freud's work). Along with this personal question, a more general one poses itself: The unconscious wish to kill the father is a special case. There are many other victims for murder in fantasy—other persons near and dear to us. The origin and the emotional consequences of such wishes are best understandable when we turn to the unconscious belief in the omnipotence of thoughts.

Taking the Will for the Deed

Freud says that he had first heard the expression "omnipotence of thought" from a very intelligent obsessional patient whom he treated. Jones, by way of correction, added that the original expression the patient used was "omnipotence of wishes." [22]

The main characteristic of that belief is an overappreciation of one's wishes, as if they could direct the course of events in the outside world. To think of someone's death means, for instance, that the person would die. This exaggerated belief in the power of one's thoughts certainly has its origin in childhood, but its traces are clearly seen in many cases of neurotics and even in the superstitions of normal people. These beliefs come to the surface especially in cases of obsession neurosis where they create fears and reaction formations as well as obsessive defense actions of the patients against their own evil wishes. These persons often experience a guilt feeling as if they had committed a murder, while in real life they would often be unable to hurt a fly. "The wicked flee when no man pursueth" says the proverb.

To choose an example close to that question of the mandarin: A young man, a patient of Freud, was shocked by the thought that his father should die so that he, the patient, would be rich enough to marry a certain woman. [23]

Someone has said that money does not make a person happy, but the lack of it certainly makes many people unhappy. From such poverty the patient for a moment saw a way out by the imagined death of his father. Most obsessional patients seek a solution of their emotional conflicts by the thought of the death of another person and often punish themselves for it, but many so-called "normal" people have similar thoughts. It is but a step from malaise to malady.

Imagining something thus becomes in such cases equivalent to doing it. One's fantasy is able to gratify his needs, but also awakens guilt feelings and anxiety if the imagined thing is, for instance, connected with the death of a dear relative. Man, a little lower than the angels, cannot, it seems, have such fantasies without self-punishment or guilt feelings. Although this seems madness at first, there is some method in it, because, as Freud declared, thinking means trial actions or actions with small quantities. Yet we all sometimes entertained that forbidden fantasy of killing someone in thought. (The man who has never had murderous thoughts in his life should be on display in Macy's window.) What, then, is that criminal's name? . . . Everyman. It was Mark Twain who said: "If desire to kill and the opportunity to kill were always together, who would escape hanging?"

Also thought murder:

> *Though it have no tongue, will speak*
> *With most miraculous organ.*

I would like to add just one example of that belief in the omnipotence of wishes to the previous ones in which the will was taken for the murderous deed.

The instance, discussed by Freud,[24] is especially informative because the idea of thought murder remained unconscious while the patient was afraid to mention death at all.

Her unconscious death wish was directed against her husband whose possible death did not appear in her thoughts. Her husband has asked someone to take his dull razors to be sharpened. The wife herself went to the store, but on returning demanded that her husband remove those razors for all time. She had discovered a store with coffins and articles of mourning near that other store. The razors got thus into a indissoluble connection with the thoughts of death. The real reason for banning the razors was, of course, her reluctance to face the unconscious wish that her husband should cut his throat with a sharpened razor.

Like the victims in Pierre Corneille's comedy,[25] the people whom those neurotic patients kill in their thoughts usually enjoy good health and long life.

Even when this is not so, there is generally a way out for the patient. I knew of a case of this kind, when a woman had a bitter argument with an old uncle and wished him dead. When the old man had a stroke a few weeks later and died, she thought that *"le bon Dieu"* had heard her prayer. She could thus shift the responsibility, and left God holding the bag.

A student I treated advanced an odd benevolent argument for his wish that his uncle should die and leave him some money. He said: "He has no enjoyment of life any longer; disease tortures him and the vital functions of his body are seriously impaired. He merely exists. Why, I believe God in His kindness makes life unpleasant and death welcome for very old people of this kind. Why should they not be released? I don't mean by murder, but by some form of euthanasia!" However, he did not forget that he would then inherit enough money to enjoy life more than heretofore.

The onset of murderous fantasies is often difficult to define. A psychologist in one of my seminars reported the case of a young man who, seeing a muscular man, often said to himself: "Could I take him? Would I win against him?" In this way he indulged in pleasurable thoughts of how he would "beat the hell out" of that man or how he would make "mince meat of him."

We shall have enough opportunity to discuss conscious and unconscious death wishes later, and we therefore return to the still unanswered question, why Freud again brought up that phrase, *"tuer son mandarin."*

Did the discussion of the omnipotence of wishes bring us any closer to the answer? No, but it is certainly interesting that Freud himself had a certain superstitious attitude toward his death. Ernest Jones reports in his biography that Freud believed he would die early. Later, Freud was afraid that he would live as long as his father, who died when he was eighty-one years old. While Freud was suffering a great deal during his last illness, he asked his physician to let him die by giving him an overdose of morphine. But as it happened, Freud lived beyond his eighty-third year. His last picture, taken in London after his arrival as a refugee from Hitler, shows him sitting at his desk, working on his last paper. He was then eighty-two.[26]

Perhaps we had better approach the problem from another point. When I once remarked to Freud during a walk that the insights he had gained in *Totem and Taboo* must have been accompanied by a feeling of triumph, he was astonished and said, "No, it was rather a wonderful clarity."

I still remember a dinner party we Viennese students gave Freud in the Prater on June 30, 1930.[27] He was, it seems, in a good mood. Yet Ernest Jones pointed out that Freud had then been filled with new doubts. In the last part of *Totem and Taboo* Freud had described the murder of the primal father by the gang of his sons. Jones pointed out to Freud that he had experienced the excitement of that deed and that his doubts marked only his emotional reaction.[28] When

Jones saw him a few days later in Vienna he asked why the author of *Interpretation of Dreams* had such doubts. Freud answered: "Then I described the wish to kill one's father, and now I have described the actual killing; after all, it is a big step from a wish to the deed."

There are, besides, definite threads running from the often interrupted work on *Dostoevsky and Parricide* to the next book, *Civilization and Its Discontents*. The fact that Freud wrote that study on Dostoevsky at the initiation of F. Eckstein and T. Fülöp-Miller did not, of course, exclude the many previous trains of thoughts expressed in it. The editors' request had no more influence on the psychological content of that article than Queen Elizabeth's wish to see Falstaff in a love adventure had on Shakespeare's *Merry Wives of Windsor*.

At the time Freud conceived *Totem and Taboo*, he declared in a letter to Jones in August, 1911: "I know I am following a crooked way in the order of my work, but it is the order of unconscious connections." [29]

When we follow that way of "unconscious connections," we can perhaps guess what reminded Freud again of Rousseau's famous mandarin in 1926 or 1927. He had passed his seventieth year.

Although he was famous, he had still many serious conflicts with his scientific adversaries as well as with his students who, like Carl Jung, had deserted him and turned against him. He sometimes felt as if he were that primal father against whom the rebellious sons ganged up and whom they wanted to kill. That phrase *"tuer son mandarin"* must have sometimes occurred to him in this connection.

Yes, the father or a father-figure is like that monster in Greek mythology, the Hydra with nine heads. When one head is stricken off, two others spring out in its place. The father, though long dead, is in this sense immortal and thus the subject of repeated attacks. The French sometimes quote a sentence of Desnoyers that one must kill the dead (*"Ce sont les morts qu'il faut qu'on tuer"*).

Interlude: Guilt Feeling and Aggression

When we discussed that strange belief in the omnipotence of wishes in which the will is taken for the dead, we remarked that various motives are operating in those murderous thoughts: want of money, competition, sexual desire, and others. One must strictly differentiate between those various motives and the nature of guilt feelings that so often follow those evil wishes. Before we proceed, we must clarify certain aspects of this problem.

We have to consider that most death wishes of that kind remain unconscious, or else, after a moment when they come to the mental surface, are energetically repressed, banned into the unconscious netherworld. They manifest themselves then only in the neurotic symptoms they create. To describe a relatively simple case: Many years ago I treated a young girl whose most conspicuous symptoms were painful sensations in or around the heart. These sensations she described as horrible, accompanied by a feeling of utter annihilation. Repeated examination of the woman by various cardiologists showed that there was no organic basis for the sensations and that they must be of a neurotic nature.

Here is the result of the psychoanalytic treatment of this patient, to make a long story short. (Other clinical cases described in this book will follow the same principle—of making long stories short.)

In my psychoanalytic sessions we investigated the various occasions on which the painful sensations were felt. These occasions had some common violent emotional reactions. She experienced, for instance, those highly unpleasant sensations when she was once tempted to steal a few stamps in her office or when she thought that she could have sexual intercourse with a young man who had wooed her. She felt those heart symptoms on an occasion when she would have liked to give another girl in the office "a piece of her mind," in reply to a sharply critical remark.

From the interpretation of some dreams and slips of the tongue, a childhood memory finally emerged. When the girl was still very young and did something "naughty," her mother, who must have been a very hysterical person, often told her: "When you behave like this, it is as if you pierced my heart with a dagger."

The origin of the heart sensations thus became transparent through introjection of the mother. It was as if thinking of certain temptations the girl unconsciously was reminded of what would have been the effect of this or that action upon her mother.

The heart sensations emerged suddenly and their cause had sometimes to be found on a long detour. To give one instance: One evening when she was in a very good mood she began to hum a melody she had heard on the radio, from Richard Rodgers' *Carousel*. Suddenly she felt such a pain in the region of the heart that she thought she would die the next minute. In the psychoanalytic session she remembered the words to that tune: "If I loved you. . . ." She must have unconsciously thought of a certain young man. The continuation of that train of thought into the unconscious is easy to guess: If I loved you, I would yield to you and go to bed with you whether you marry me or not. The connection of that thought possibility with the imagined reaction of her mother is easily conjectured.

The task of the psychoanalyst in cases of this kind is obvious. He has to bring the underlying feeling of guilt to the surface of consciousness. He must, so to speak, lift the stone and see what is under it. As long as the guilt feeling is unconscious and expresses itself only in self-damaging actions or sensations, it cannot be dealt with.

Such a transformation of a subterraneous sense of guilt into a conscious one, is, of course, connected with a transitory depression of the patient, but this cannot be avoided. One cannot spare him from that short unpleasant emotion.

One has to consider that the depression was already unconsciously present and the transformation did not change its character or only as far as a negative in a photographic picture is changed to a positive. The advantage of that change is clear: The psychoanalytic "working through" of that guilt feeling presents the excellent possibility of mastering it, of its psychological conquest. Such emotional mastery is facilitated by the insight that most persons with vivid murderous fantasies could, in actuality, not kill a fly; it would get away while it was being chased.

One of the most important insights given us by psychoanalysis is the understanding of the origin and character of that guilt feeling. It is the result of the work of the later years of Freud and has a revolutionary character because it removed the assumption that guilt feelings originate in sexuality.

Freud has enabled us to comprehend that guilt feelings always have their roots in aggressive trends whose continuation into the unconscious leads to murderous wishes.[30] This assumption about the origin of the sense of guilt permits no exception and is as pervasive and determined as the laws of physics and chemistry.

The critical objection anticipated here will, of course, point to the obvious connection of guilt feelings with forbidden sexual activities. To take an instance near at hand: An adolescent boy masturbates and feels guilty about it. It is obvious that this feeling is related with masturbation. The only question is, how is it related? Psychoanalytic exploration shows that the connection exists, but that the boy has omitted a very essential unconscious middle thought or feeling. It is this: If now my father (or mother) would come in and would interrupt me or reproach me on account of that forbidden act, I would be so furious that I could attack him. Thus the guilt feeling corresponds not to the masturbation directly, but to the violent and murderous repressed impulses of the boy.

The same dynamics govern other cases of other forbidden sexual activities. A married woman who had a long-standing affair with a man felt very guilty toward her husband. In reality she felt guilty because she unconsciously wished him to die so that he would not disturb her relationship with her lover. If one does not distinctly differentiate between the sexual and the aggressive trends in those cases, the danger is not so much that a fusion of the two emotional powers results, but that a confusion is the consequence.

Let me insert here two short case histories. An engineer came into psychoanalytic treatment because he suffered from stomach ache, flatulence, and many other symptoms. The physicians who examined him declared that his complaints were of a neurotic character. He was all the more lonely because he was afraid that the smell of wind would make him impossible in company. In his office also he was socially isolated. There was the occasion when he expressed vehement criticism of his boss upon whom he heaped personal and vicious abuse and curses. To his astonishment, his flatulence disappeared and his previous hypochondrial complaints receded, especially when he wished that the boss should fall dangerously ill.

The other case I would like to mention shows the rare and penetrating insight of a woman into the unconscious motives of her husband. She knew that he had been having a long extramarital affair and she recognized that he would have liked to get a divorce from her. Being a mother of three small children, she foresaw that her husband would not provide enough money for their education, and she was unyieldingly reluctant to agree to a divorce.

When the husband's car was being repaired, he borrowed his wife's small car to drive from their suburban home to the city. He smashed this car, which he had given her many years ago. Since he was a tricky lawyer, he succeeded in getting another small car through insurance. A few days later he also wrecked the new car.

She boldly declared in her analytic sessions: "The car is, of course, his unconscious representation of me. He would like to kill me and instead of this he has twice demolished my car."

This interpretation sounds at first irrational, but makes good sense when you consider the psychological situation in which this couple lives. I could not contradict her, especially since, in the language of dreams, cars really represent women. (A child is inside a woman. Also, taxi drivers often call their car "she.")

How important the unconscious guilt feelings in the case of neurotic patients is, and how urgent its transformation and conquest, will be understood only after one recognizes the part unconscious self-damage and self-punishment have in the vicissitudes of other patients. Here is the stage man-

ager behind the wings in many human tragedies. We shall
follow a few representative instances of this kind later on.

We may as well be prepared to consider that part of the
unconscious guilt feeling in a much wider frame, beyond
that of the individual life: in the history of mankind. In
Civilization and Its Discontents Freud wrote: "I suspect the
reader feels that the discussion about the sense of guilt over-
steps its proper boundaries in this essay. . . . But it faith-
fully corresponds to my intention to represent the sense of
guilt as the most important problem in the evolution of culture." This sentence was quoted as an epigraph to a previous
book of mine.[31] It will be remembered later when we discuss
the role of the sense of guilt following murderous plans in
the life of groups. We shall cross the bridge to the psychology of groups when we come to it.

One's Own Experience

The French have a saying that one always returns to one's
first loves. Is it also true that one always returns to the problems he was confronted with and with which he had to grapple in his youth? It seems so. The "life review," as a psychiatrist has recently characterized a natural, mental experience
in the aged,[32] shows a harking back to certain past experiences, seen perhaps in new light.

When we look into a mirror we see a stranger. Only by a
successful evasion of oneself, only by not seeing ourselves as

if we were strangers do we not see that we are all potential murderers. That "life review" was actualized in my own case by a coronary attack early in 1960. The long recovery process was accompanied by a review of past experiences, especially of the one connected with my father's death when I was eighteen years old.

Freud once stated that an experience that was written down will be mastered, emotionally conquered. This is correct to a certain degree, but perhaps only a great writer, as Freud was, or a great poet, can describe or narrate deep-reaching experiences beyond that degree. When I was not yet twenty-six years old—before I went into personal psychoanalysis in Berlin—I tried to relive and review that experience in an article, written in 1913 and published anonymously in the *Psychoanalytische Zeitschrift* in 1914. Its title was *On the Effects of Unconscious Death Wishes*.[33] It was the first of my longer articles in that journal, edited by Freud. Until then, only some of my short reviews had appeared in it.

Only thirty-five years later, in 1949, did I dare to publish a detailed report about my youthful experience. It was in the book, *Fragment of a Great Confession,* which was conceived as a psychoanalytic autobiography.[34]

But there was, in that youthful paper written in 1913, the raw material, so to speak, of that experience, remembered and revived without consideration for its artistic or stylistic form and formulation. (It was also not accidental that the dedication of the book, *Fragment of a Great Confession*, reads as follows: "In memory of my teacher and friend Sigmund Freud on the tenth anniversary of his death, September 1949.")

My father died of a heart attack when I was eighteen years old. The image of the man who sat in an easy chair and had great breathing difficulties followed me for many months. I was ordered to run to the pharmacy to get camphor for an injection. In the part of Vienna in which we then lived, neither taxi nor bus was available. I knew how important the injection was. I ran through streets as if for my life, but it was for his life. To catch my breath I had to stop sometimes, and then run the more quickly. I knew—or thought I knew—that the life of my father depended on my speed. It was, so to speak, a race with death. At a certain moment the thought occurred to me that my father was already dead. I reached the pharmacy, got the medicine, and rushed home. When I burst into our apartment, I knew even before I saw him that my father was dead. As if struck by an electric shock, I threw myself on his body to kiss him and to get his pardon.

The following weeks were filled with mourning, but also with remorse. At times that moment when I had to stop for breath came to mind, with the awful question: If I had run faster could I not have saved my father's life?

Yet, strangely enough, that remorse or thought was sometimes interrupted by a kind of revolt against the dead man, as if in repetition of previous rebellious tendencies; I had the feeling of having been abandoned by him and as if he had wanted to leave me. He had no right to do this, it occurred to me, until my younger sister and I could fend for ourselves. I understood, of course, how absurd those thoughts were, but I could not suppress them.

To my despair, a wave of sexual excitement overpowered me during many sleepless nights. I appeared to myself then as a kind of monster. When, a few weeks afterward, I found occasion to have sexual intercourse, I was seized with horror at myself. On the other hand, I experienced an intense and impassioned ambition which I had not felt—at least not consciously—until then. It was as if I had to achieve something extraordinary to atone for my death wish against the dear man, but also to make his name famous. (Why does the biblical phrase "to sanctify thy name" occur to me?)

My father had been a railway inspector and was often addressed as "Mr. Inspector," and this word came frequently to mind as if I thought that he would inspect, examine what I did and what I thought.

In this way I projected again into the outside world—even into the world beyond this one—the power and the knowledge of the superego that knows what takes place in the area of drives and desires.

If I had known Freud's *Civilization and Its Discontents*, I would have understood that thoughts could not remain secret before the superego that punishes the person.[35] The difference between doing something evil and wishing to do it no longer exists in this phase of development. The superego does not acknowledge that difference and fills the ego with anxiety. The superego thus really takes the will for the deed.

Much of this, including my youthful dreams of glory— alas, never to be realized—I described in that book, published in 1949, and I do not want to repeat myself, because it would be a thrice-told tale. That book, as its title indicates, is the fragment of a great confession.

Since that autobiographical analysis, the memory of that moment when I rested for some minutes from my race to the pharmacy rarely returned. It was as if I had really emotionally conquered the experience that had tortured me for a long time, by means of the confession within that book.

Yet since 1949 there have been a few times when that old memory came back to mind. One was during my coronary attack in 1960, or rather, during the first phase of the recovery process. There were some minutes of breathlessness or difficulty in breathing, in which the image of my dying father emerged. And then followed for a moment the memory of dashing through the streets of Vienna to the pharmacy. Those moments were accompanied by fear of dying.

During the first weeks after father's death, attacks of re-taliation fear for my evil fantasies against him were frequent and intense. They slowly receded and by and by grew weaker, until they emerged again many years later—as a matter of fact, at an age several years beyond that which my father reached.

Unconscious death wishes of the son against the father are, it seems, inevitable and fated, but such are retaliation fears of the son. One is tempted to vary that biblical sentence to the effect that fate visits the sins against the father upon the children unto all following generations. The sky is no limit for those wishes to kill others. The gods and goddesses of almost all religions have evil designs against each other and against human beings.

Seventy-Six Years Old

In *Fragment of a Great Confession* I treated fully the rela-tionship with my first wife, Ella, and her illness. I discussed also the mysterious attack of sudden and alarming dizziness I often experienced whenever I visited her in the sanatorium where she was being treated. When I was almost fifty years old, I returned to psychoanalysis for a few weeks. Freud ex-plained those attacks to me; they were reactions to emerging death wishes against my wife. The unconscious wish that she should die, after having been ill so long, had been turned against myself and had produced that dizziness together with the feeling of imminent annihilation.

After Ella's death, I married my second wife, Maria, who was much younger than I. She was born in Derwental in Bosnia, then a province of the Austria-Hungarian monarchy. I had passed through that place on horseback during the First World War when she was a little girl. Maria gave me two lovely daughters, Irene and Miriam, and we were happy during the first years after we arrived in the United States in 1938, having escaped from Holland, then already endangered by the Nazis. Miriam was born in New York.

A few years later, the first symptoms of a serious illness were observed in Maria. After many examinations and tests, there was no further doubt possible; it was multiple sclerosis, an incurable disease. In the following years the organic disease was aggravated and my wife became permanently incapacitated. Her paralysis made it necessary to feed her, to wash and clean her. She was brought to a nursing home where she spent several years until her death on Christmas, 1959.

I am convinced that it was not accidental that I had my coronary attack a few days after her death. I know that I must often have wished that she should die, and my coronary attack was the reaction to her death—a self-punishment, almost reaching self-annihilation. It was not only atonement and self-punishment; I must have loved her more than I knew. I shall perhaps get around to that later, but first I would like to speak of something else.

In May, 1964, I reached the age of seventy-six, and some weeks later my sister and I moved into an apartment on West 86th Street. (My son Arthur lives opposite us.)

I became gradually habituated to the new surroundings and sometimes observed people, while sitting at the window when I did not feel like reading or writing. On the other side of the street was the Bentley School, an excellent private school, as I learned later on. (The tuition is not low.) While our apartment was being tidied, I sat at the window after breakfast and saw the school boys and girls arriving around eight-thirty. A father always brings his daughter to school in his car, and somewhat enviously I thought that I never had a car. The psychological differences of the sexes are easily recognizable. The girls have more, and more vivid, gestures than the boys. When a boy waits for a comrade and another young man passes by, the waiting boy is not interested and looks away. A girl in the same situation, seeing another young woman, usually looks her over, but good—hat, dress, stockings, shoes. There are four steps up to the school where people go in and out. The male students unhesitatingly sit on them when they have nothing else to do, but I never saw a girl sit there, unless she first put down some newspapers, or in any case some books to sit on. (Girls pull their skirts down after being seated. In conversation with boys, girls seem to be more animated but they are better at concealing their personal interest in the partner than boys.)

These and other observations are, of course, made in the spirit of cool theoretical interest of a psychologist, but—strangely enough—they are sometimes accompanied, yes, even interrupted, by a mysterious feeling of bitterness—or is it envy? I suddenly catch myself experiencing a kind of morbid hate for all those young people, a sharp secret envy. "They have everything," I say; "they are young and they have a future. I am old and I have nothing to look forward to."

In general my mood in those weeks following my seventy-sixth birthday was one of discouragement and depression. It was the spring of my discontent. I tried to escape that mood by taking a walk, and then and there I decided to visit my younger daughter Miriam who lived not far away. She of-

fered me coffee, but I refused and began to talk. I told her
that I had been feeling depressed and was often thinking
how I had wronged some people and hurt their feelings,
and I perhaps felt poignant remorse—now when it was
much too late to do anything about it. And then I began to
talk about Miriam's mother. I had often been cruelly incon-
siderate to her and often short and impulsively abrupt, perhaps even offensive. It was a kind of shameful confession
poured out, but without humility.

I told Miriam that I must have made her mother suffer.
(Did I suffer too? I don't know.) I confessed to Miriam that
I had not often visited her mother in the nursing home
where she spent her last years, that I had neglected Maria
more and more; yes, that there were many days when I did
not even think of her. I worked and enjoyed life; I slept with
other women—I had almost forgotten that I had an incura-
bly ill wife in a nursing home not very far from where I
lived. When the thought of her occurred, I sometimes felt
ashamed, but I nevertheless did not visit her. I sometimes
fooled myself into believing that perhaps she did not even
want to see me. But I knew, of course, that this was not
true—at least during the first months at that nursing home
on West End Avenue.

All this I told Miriam. It was a moment, or rather an hour,
of truth—"all my sins remembered," as with Hamlet. It was
not only a confession, but also a self-accusation; but,
strangely enough, told and formulated without emotion,
as if I spoke of the omissions and mistakes of a stranger,
yes, like a prosecutor speaking of the deeds of a defendant.

I knew all the while I was speaking that Miriam had been
aware of all my omissions and mistakes for years, since she
visited her mother in that nursing home as often as possible.
She must have often wondered about the strange behavior of
her father and must have accused him of neglecting her

mother. Now she sat opposite me, listening and not saying a word.

Toward evening I said, "I must go now." I kissed my daughter; she accompanied me to the door, waiting while I rang the bell for the elevator. When the elevator arrived at the floor, Miriam said, "One must forgive oneself too."

Walking home, I wondered about this daughter of mine. From where had she got this wisdom? My depression receded by and by, as I walked through the streets in the calm of the evening. It was like coming out of a tunnel. I repeated to myself, "One must forgive oneself too."

The Secret Communication

Françoise Mallet-Joris remarks in a recent book[36] that the well-known phrase, "It is always the best who leave us,"— a phrase that does not carry much conviction—is often spoken at deathbeds. The writer points to the fact that the dead have become harmless, as a partial explanation of that saying.

Fifty-five years ago, E. W. Howe, known as "the Sage of Potato Hill," wrote "When a man dies and his kin are glad of it, they say: 'He is better off.'" [37] (Don't they sometimes say this before the death, perhaps in the conditional form, that he would be better off dead?) But this would imply a conscious wish, and we are especially interested in the origin and character of unconscious death wishes, or at least of those that reach the mental surface for a split second to be energetically repressed. We are, of course, also deeply interested in the emotional reactions produced by those murderous wishes.

In the halls of the Vienna University is the statue of the famous surgeon Nothnagel. His oft-quoted saying, "Only a good man can be a good physician," is engraved beneath. In the light of depth psychology this means: Only he who has mastered and transformed his original cruel and brutal tendencies into benevolent and human feeling can become a good physician. That saying cannot deny the original barbarous and bloodthirsty impulses of man. It only concedes the possibility of their transformation. And indignant denial of that primal human character could only reveal the fact that, as Albert Camus expressed it, "Man is the only creature who refuses to be what he is."

How are those trends conveyed to the psychotherapist? Are they conveyed to him at all, since they are deeply submerged in the unconscious? We unfalteringly trust in Freud's early statement that mortals are not made to keep secrets.

The analyst's effort to understand these unconscious wishes is, it is true, not simple or easy, but when he achieves his aim, it almost always marks new avenues to the patient's problems. Very rarely, breakthroughs from the area of the repressed occur, and then the whole emotional landscape is suddenly put in a new strong light. Often enough the analyst must laboriously reconstruct a forgotten past exactly as an archaeologist constructs an ancient temple from its ruins, a few pillars and columns.

I was told of a little girl who said, "Throwing up is hard for children." It is often just as hard for some adult patients to confess death wishes toward their parents or other relatives. Yet the total absence of such violent impulses or thoughts in an extended psychoanalytic treatment is as conspicuous as (to keep within the area of mystery stories) the non-barking of a dog in a Sherlock Holmes story.

I once treated a teacher who gave the impression of quiet meekness. It seemed he was afraid of expressing even slight annoyance or impatience. Yet much later he unconsciously revealed that he was full of aggressive and murderous wishes —in this case against the children in his class.

It is sometimes enough for certain patients to see an arrogant or presumptuous man to awaken their aggressive tendencies. In the following fantasies remarkable examples of American know-how come to the surface. The train of thought starts from the sentence, "Who does he think he is?" and passes to aggressive wishes such as, "I would like to throw this glass of winc into his face" (simultaneously regretting the waste of good wine) and "I would like to cut him up in little pieces and flush him down the toilet." Most people who have such evil designs are far from being troublemakers. They make trouble only for themselves. Many of them are afraid of their own violent and aggressive tendencies, quite unnecessarily. They behave like horses who take fright at their own shadows. To pursue the simile, many men and women have blinders and blink at their own fantasies.

Generalizations are, of course, also false in the area of psychology. There are quite a few men who take the office troubles out on the little woman and who, returning home, start to quarrel with their wives. The death wishes they then picture against their spouses are really directed against the boss and were merely transferred to the wives.

As a marginal remark, here is an example of violent anger rising to the surface in a woman after a quarrel with her husband. She sobbed and muttered, "I'll hit him and scratch him. Oh, I'll handle him . . . !" She felt herself blushing at this point and broke off.

I am excluding from this survey the cases in which violent fantasies are mixed with the idea of rape, a subject that Dr. Ludwig Eidelberg discussed lucidly in his book, *The Dark Urge,* published in 1961.

We are, of course, prepared for the fact that murderous wishes will emerge not only against one's father, but also against one's mother, sisters, brothers, and other relatives. Most persons in psychoanalytic treatment give themselves away by slips of the tongue, by dreams whose interpretations penetrate the distortions of the surface, and even by forgetfulness concerning names.

Here are examples of this kind, remembered from analytic practice in Vienna. A man told a friend that his aunt had bequeathed a beautiful apartment house to him in her will. By a slip of the tongue, he said he hoped that the house was free of apothecaries. This sounds meaningless, but when analyzed, it makes sense. What he wanted to say was that he hoped that the house was free of "mortgages," which was the word he wanted to use for the Austrian expression *Hypothek,* much like the German *Apotheke.* Instead of saying that he hoped that the house he would once inherit was free of mortgages, he really said, was free of apothecaries (pharmacies). The unconscious meaning of the slip of the tongue became clear in a psychoanalytic session. The man had repressed the wish to poison his kind aunt (with drugs, bought at a pharmacy) in order to come into the inheritance immediately.

Here let me add an example in which the secret death fantasy revealed itself by the conspicuous forgetting of a name. A girl who had been my patient always forgot the name of the street in which her boy friend lived. The name was Bleicher Street. The analytic exploration took its point of departure from the German word *bleich,* meaning pale.

Her thought associations led her then to phrases such as "ghastly pale" and "deadly pale."

No great sagacity was needed to conclude that the memory of an incident in which her boy friend had deeply hurt her pride interfered with her knowing the name of the street where he lived. The train of thought associations followed by her left no doubt that she had indulged in vehement death fantasies against him since that incident. The only reaction the girl remembered from this scene was that, leaving her boy friend, she had murmured "Go to hell!"—which may or may not be conceived as a death wish.

For the conception of paleness as unconsciously representing death, for instance, the interpretation of the Bassanio scene in *The Merchant of Venice,* in Freud's essay "The Theme of the Three Caskets," [38] Bassanio chooses the leaden casket and addresses it with the words:

> *Thy paleness moves me more than eloquence. . . .*

Freud interprets the paleness of the lead as characteristic of death. Conspicuous paleness of persons appears also in dreams as a death symbol.

Such evil thoughts are certainly the gentlest art of murder, committed by "a dagger of the mind," to quote Shakespeare again.

One would assume that the other form of communication of those secret wishes, namely, the dream, would be even more difficult to unravel than the psychopathological phenomena of everyday life, such as slips of the tongue. In reality dreams sometimes betray much more freely death wishes of the dreamer.

In the following paragraphs I present two dreams and their interpretations. The dream occurred in 1909, when I was twenty-one years old and was published in the Munich magazine *März* (March) in 1911.[39] This was the dream's content: "I receive a telegram from Ella with the words, Jacob died. Come immediately."

At that time I was a student at the Vienna University and was in love with Ella, who later became my wife. I could not remember any person named Jacob. When I arrived a few hours after the dream, at the university, it immediately occurred to me that today I must attend a lecture of Professor Jacob Minor, who taught history of German literature. The superficial meaning of the dream thus becomes clear; if Jacob Minor is dead, I can go to K——, a town half an hour's distance from Vienna, and see Ella. I need not, then, stay at the university and was free to visit my sweetheart. Here we have a simple wish fulfillment.

Yet there must also be some significance that Ella herself wired me the news. Later it occurred to me that Jacob Minor and Ella's father had certain common characteristics in speech and behavior. My future father-in-law had his own reasons for not approving of social visits of young men at his home. I could see Ella only when he was away on a trip. "Jacob" in my dream is, so to speak, the disguised figure behind whom Ella's father appears, and when I get the news from her that he is dead and I can visit Ella.

The second dream: A patient of a colleague of mine, Dr. Adolph C. Woltman, had a dream that had the characteristics of a nightmare. The young patient had been in psychoanalytic treatment a few years before, but it was interrupted on account of the war and he had to serve. He had been overseas and had then returned to his studies in New York. The nightmare frightened him to such an extent that it brought him back into psychoanalysis.

Here is that terrifying dream:

"I was ordered to Sing Sing to execute a condemned person. I see the condemned man. As I take a second look I see that my father is strapped in the electric chair. Next to him is a physician who nods his head in a friendly way, indicating that I should throw the switch in order to kill this man. The only thing I can remember is that my father looked at me with very sad eyes."

After the patient left, Dr. Woltman jotted down the dream content as well as the description of the emotional reactions the patient experienced after awakening. He described them thus: "I woke up with a start, felt hot and drenched with sweat. My heart was beating out of my mouth. I jumped out of bed and ran into the living room, opened the window, and sat by the open window for about an hour. The time was about four o'clock in the morning. I had a terrific case of tachycardia. I clutched my chest with both hands. I was sure that my heart would stop and I would die. After suffering great anxiety for about an hour, my heart slowed down to normal. However, I was afraid to go back to bed and sat in the chair next to the open window till daylight."

I might add that the patient, until this dream emerged, had never experienced a conscious death wish toward his father. It is essential for the interpretation of this dream that the excessive rapidity of the heart action the patient described belongs to the latent dream content. It is as if he himself is the condemned man, thus both executioner and executed. ("I was sure that . . . I would die.") The unbearable anxiety also expresses this retaliation fear that torments him.

Dreams in which resentment against the psychoanalyst emerge are common. Here is an example: A patient dreams that he is in an airplane and sits beside the pilot, who shows him certain landscapes below. The patient does not like the scenery. He suddenly grasps the pilot and throws him out of the plane. The pilot is, of course, the psychoanalyst.

I am grateful to Dr. Woltman for the following example. Joe, born and brought up in South Africa nearly twenty years old, was severely crippled emotionally, Dr. Woltman reports: "At one time during the analysis I ran into serious resistance. Joe was fed up with analysis and wanted to go home. During this time he told me a fantasy which he had had the previous day. In this fantasy he saw himself back in South Africa. He saw there that New York City would be attacked with atomic weapons which would level the city completely and kill all the inhabitants. This was, of course, a disguised way in which he tried to kill me. In order not to make his death wishes toward me too obvious, he fantasied about destruction of a whole area and its inhabitants in the hope that I would be one of the victims. When I interpreted this fantasy to him, he smiled and remarked that I had seen right through his scheme to eliminate me. During the ensuing discussion he was able to verbalize his death wishes toward me. This broke the resistance, and analysis after that took on a more positive character."

The reader will be prepared to encounter the existence of unconscious death wishes in various cloaks and deceptive disguises which conceal their existence. Such misleading appearances correspond to an "unconscious alibi," if that's the word I want. The analyst treating cases of various kinds sometimes sees such hidden wishes suddenly emerge where he would least suspect them. In general, originality of observation is more important than accuracy. You notice, for instance, a single odd feature, a false gesture, or emphasis on a wrong syllable in an everyday report of the patient, and consider them revealing. Analysis may well start here, and psychoanalysis means that the patient becomes acquainted with a stranger, namely, himself. That is the case even where some emotional piece was previously guessed in the patient. Yet knowing something unconscious and being told about it, brought to the conscious mind by another person, are psychologically two different things.

Before we turn our attention to the variety and multiplicity of unconscious death wishes met with in psychoanalytic treatment of neurotic patients, a sidelong glance at the psychology of children will be necessary. Children have their contradictory feelings and conflicts just as we do. In a novel by the German writer Heinrich Boell (born 1917) a man makes the comment old people are wrong in speaking of "the happy age of youth; when one was young, everything was serious and difficult, and no one helped you."

The Kids

We are accustomed to imagine that death wishes are eruptions of hatred, envy and jealousy; which means they are full of emotions. Many are, of course, and resemble in this way Beethoven's *Sonata appassionata*. They are full of fury, but there are others, daydreams of almost a poetic character comparable to the *Moonlight Sonata* and others of a casual, distant, emotionless nature—finger exercises, so to speak.

How different from those of adults are children's thoughts of this kind. Looking at some persons, it is difficult to imagine that they were children. But is it not also difficult to conceive of ourselves as little boys and girls? The ideas children have of death are, of course, far different from ours. When my son Arthur, who will soon be fifty years old, was a little boy, he used to tell me, "Be a little dead!" when he wanted me to leave the room for some time. This wish, of course, didn't exclude my returning after some minutes.

Yet we find among children the same emotions that lead grown-ups to death wishes. An old aunt whom we used to visit on a Sunday forenoon promised my little sister Margaret that she would leave her a beautiful golden watch in her will. Margaret must have become impatient, because she once asked her aunt, "When do you die already?" (In ungrammatical German, *"Wann sterbst du schon?"*)

Emotions originating in the Oedipus situation express themselves in early childhood with sudden vehemence. A patient of Bernard Berkowitz reported a little scene with his daughter, not yet three years old. The child had wandered into the parents' bedroom one Sunday morning when the parents were already awake but still in bed. She came to the side where her mother lay and began to beat her mother with clenched fists. She took her mother's arm and wanted to pull her out of the bed. All the while the little girl kept crying, "My daddy, my daddy!"

Mildred Newman-Berkowitz told me of a seven-year-old girl who dreamed that her friend's mother had died. The dreamer danced in the funeral procession to the tune of a minuet. She knew that she looked beautiful and was happy. When she awoke, she understood immediately it was her own mother and felt deeply ashamed about being so happy in her dream.

I am grateful to Mildred also for the communication of the following anecdote: A boy of four was riding with his mother on a bus. He asked his mother who would die sooner, she or he. His mother explained that older persons usually die before children. Twenty minutes later, mother and child had to get off the bus. Walking to the door, the boy said with loud, triumphant voice: "All people in this bus will die before me." A brief interval of time was sufficient to transform that nice little boy into a monster.

More often than we believe, children think of the death of nearest relatives in order to keep a secret from them. There are two examples of this kind in my practice. Little Sylvia had heard that her father had been married before and had married her mother only after the death of his first wife. The girl imagined that her mother did not know this and was anxious to conceal it since she thought that her mother's pride would be very much hurt if she learned of it. She wished her father would die before the secret became known.

Sarah was the daughter of a rabbi, who taught a number of older students. One of them came often to the house when the rabbi was away and played sexually with the little girl. Sarah was very much ashamed of it, but did not dare to resist the older man, a favorite student of her father's. What worried her most of all was that her father could come to know about this sexual play and she wished he would die before this news reached him. When the rabbi died, the daughter felt no grief but rather somewhat relieved from the burden of her secret.

Freud analyzed a childhood memory of Goethe.[40] The boy amused himself and the citizens of Frankfurt am Main when he threw many plates and pots from the window to the street. He showed by this action that he wanted to get rid of his baby brother Jacob, just then born. Johann Wolfgang was almost ten years old when his younger brother died. According to Bettina Brentano,[41] his mother considered it strange that the boy did not cry after Jacob's death, although the youngster had been his playmate. Instead, he seemed to be annoyed by the laments of his sister and brother.

Freud himself mentions in a letter to Fliers the evil wishes he, then a little older than Goethe in that scene, had felt against his younger brother Julius.

A patient of mine remembered wishing a teacher dead when she was in elementary school; she had memorized her lesson well but had not been called upon to recite. She also wished for the death of her father when he did not take her to a movie. She recalled this when the father really died. She was then twelve years old. It was perhaps advantageous that such death wishes occurred to Freud's patient, a grown woman, at most insignificant occasions. For instance, she applied for the job as a secretary; the lawyer who interviewed her kept looking at some legal documents on his desk. She immediately wished him dead because he did not "give me his undivided attention."

We cannot here enter into a discussion of the factors determining the transformation of puberty and their influence upon violent impulses. In one of his recent novels, *Les Inconnus dans le maison,* Georges Simenon describes a juvenile gang of thieves in a small French town. An unknown man is found murdered in the house of the lawyer Loursat. The lawyer defends a member of the gang, Robert Mann. The president of the court asks another member whether there was any discussion about killing the man who exploited them. Maître Loursat gets restless because no one wanted to understand the language of these young people. "They could have discussed even the minutest details of the crime and it would all have ended there. They created the drama to amuse themselves." Unfortunately, in this particular case the fantasy became reality. One of the juvenile gang really killed the man.

Long before Simenon's novel, a French writer, Marquis de Sade pointed out in his *Justine* (1791) the danger implied in the transition from daydream to the deed:

> *"The dream dissipated were once to recover one's medi-
> ocre import—'tis story of moral wrongdoing. Everyone
> knows very well and it offends no one. But alas, one
> sometimes carries the thing a little further. What one
> does wonder, what would not be the idea's realization,
> if its mere abstract shape thus evoked has just so pro-
> foundly moved one? The accursed reverie is vivified
> and its existence is a crime?"*

But we are tempted to follow those psychological transformations while we wished only to cast some light on the
nature of children's death wishes. It is a long way from that
infantile chase to the fantasy life of grown-ups. However, it
was instructive to look into the realm of childhood impulses
and thoughts. Besides, a thousand-mile journey begins with
a single step.

I avail myself of this opportunity to add a favorite piece
of theory concerning the character of murderous fantasies.
I believe that those violent wishes have many earmarks of
children's impulses and thoughts. This belief should, of
course, not excuse them, but make us understand them
better. The passions and impulses of childhood are just as
vehement as those of adults, but they are short-lived and
their intensity soon evaporates. You say you hate someone
like poison or like sin? Such phrases would not occur to a
child.

Children's murderous thoughts also show a different concept of death. Children conceive of death as sleep (an echo
of it can be found even in Hamlet's soliloquy) or as a temporary absence which does not exclude the return of the
person. (One could reverse the French phrase: *"Mourir
c'est partir un peu."*) Children lack the means of killing that
are at the disposal of grown-up persons. In their fantasies
the means are sometimes surprisingly harmless.

With children, death has not the finality that we connect with the idea. They do not imagine the agony of dying, the suffocation of the last hour, the death struggle. Their fantasies concerning dying has therefore the character of unreality. It seems to me that the belief in the omnipotence of wishes of which Freud speaks is greatest in childhood and later on gradually diminished.

Considering those characteristic features and observing that remnants of them survive also in murderous fantasies later on, we wonder whether one ever really becomes an adult.

Forgotten Childhood Verses Return

As far as I know, no book on psychoanalysis has yet dealt with the subject of false confessions, so well known to criminologists. Not many instances are publicized in which innocent people have "confessed" to murder. Such cases would not be possible if those people were not potentially murderers in thought. They are made possible by a confusion of daydream and reality.

Murderous impulses sometimes emerge for a split second and vanish; others remain, and many even acquire the character of delusions. If we psychologists were in possession of something like x-ray, we would certainly recognize uncommitted crimes that were nipped in the bud.

We are accustomed to connect murderous impulses with

great passions, with envy and desire, with frustrated ambition and greed, and we rarely imagine that an insignificant motive can be responsible for violent fantasies. I would like to give an example of such a wish that occurred only yesterday. It matters little that the murderous fantasy was mine.

Here is the prehistory of this little piece of self-analysis. My sister Margaret was in Lake Placid Hospital, being treated for anemia. I had visited her there and heard with great satisfaction that her condition was improving and that she would soon leave the hospital.

Grete, as I call her, has never married, and manages my household, as she has done for many years. I know how devoted she is to me and often how self-sacrificing she is in the interests of making our home as comfortable as possible for me. Her kindness is natural and never self-conscious.

When I returned from the hospital, I was astonished at being haunted by children's verses running through my mind. I am sure I had not thought of them in seventy or more years. At first only the beginning line occurred to me. Here is the German text, as far as I could recall. I am not sure that it is altogether correct.

> Mariechen sass auf einen Stein, einen Stein, einen Stein;
> Da kam der Bruder Karl her.
> "Mariechen, warum weinest du, weinest du?"
> "Weil ich heute sterben muss."
> Da stach Karl Mariechen in das Herz.
> Mariechen war ein Engelein,
> Und Karl war ein Bengelein."

> (*Little Mary sat on a stone, on a stone, on a stone;*
> *Her brother Karl came in then.*
> *"Little Mary why do you cry, do you cry?"*

"Because today I have to die."
Karl ran a dagger into Mary's heart.
Mary was a little angel,
But Karl was a little rascal.")

Why did brother Karl kill little Mary? We don't know. The poem does not tell us. Like Iago's, his evil design seems motiveless—simply a motiveless homicidal passion.

At all events, we are not interested in Karl's psychology but in mine. Why did that old children's song, heard so often when I was a little boy in Vienna's Augarten (a park) occur to me? Why had I suddenly recalled the theme of this childrens' song? It haunted me. Was I perhaps that evil brother Karl?

I rejected the idea. My sister is called Grete, not Mary, and my name is not Karl. And yet. . . . I am in no way aware that I wanted to kill Grete, and yet that song kept haunting me.

Something occurred to me but I do not think this was what I was searching for, because it would be ludicrous, ridiculous—and yet. . . . Grete is a few years younger than I and does not want me to smoke after coffee. She insists that she cannot tolerate the smell, and I always have to wait until later before I can smoke.

Since she has been in the hospital a little more than a week, I light my cigarette even before the coffee is served.

My pen refuses to write it, but it is useless to resist. I must have resented it bitterly, "murderously," that I could not smoke at the table. It is not clear to me that Grete's opposition to my smoking provoked such violent and vehement feelings of hatred toward her. There were—I well recall—other occasions during our childhood when she made me furious—why then should that children's song have occurred to me? When I returned from the hospital the memory of those old murderous impulses must have occurred to me when I had my lunch and could smoke as much as I liked.

There is no need here to unravel the strands of childhood memories. I hope that this little incident will convince the reader that trivial or commonplace occasions may often lead to murderous fantasies. We are all influenced by forces beyond our control. Yet one has to come to terms with one's past, and one has to face the future, however brief it may be.

A petty annoyance that began in my impatience to smoke may well lead to violent wishes like those I must have had toward Grete, of whom I am very fond. In other relationships greed, unfair competition, and many other motives may turn the most intimate friends into the direst enemies.

From Psychoanalytic Experiences

A few years ago, Henry A. Murray sarcastically remarked that psychologists are undertaking Satan's task of shattering man's faith in his own potentialities. He says that "if we psychologists were all the time consciously or unconsciously intending out of malice to reduce the concept of human nature to its largest common denominators, then we might have to admit that to this extent the Satanic spirit was alive within us." [42]

The objection provoked by those remarks (not to mention the distaste produced by the theological language in scientific discussion), will point to the part of guilt feelings and of the superego, to be evaluated elsewhere in this chapter.

When I read Murray's address, I was reminded of an acquaintance of mine, a man of eighty-two, who, I knew, suffered a number of serious complaints related to old age. I once encountered him on the street and told him that he looked well. The answer was, "Yes, there is nothing wrong with my face."

If we psychologists could judge only by appearance, we would also come to the conclusion that there is nothing wrong with human nature. But it is not our task to use the illimitable freedom of the human mind "and to follow truth wherever it may lead," to quote Jefferson's words at his dedication of the University of Virginia.

They say that the motives for murder are not very numerous; love, jealousy, desire for money, ambition. The same motives are to be found at the bottom of thought murders or of murderous fantasies. (We need not mention means and opportunities that play such a decisive part in real murders, since we are venturing in the area of fantasy, where everything can be said and done.)

My impression is that in the few cases of a "murder in the mind," touched upon in the preceding section, that we were remote from the area of the phrase, *"tuer son mandarin,"* that had been our point of departure.

It is not difficult, however, to find cases which are much closer to it, although individual features are different.

I owe the following example to my colleague Benjamin Margolis. The particular feature of this case is that the patient was entirely unaware that certain thoughts of hers had the character of a death wish. The woman had gone through a severe emotional conflict with her husband. She had considered divorcing him when it occurred to her that he was heavily insured. Continuing this train of thought, she arrived at the idea how beautiful life would be for her and her child if she came into possession of that sizable amount of money.

Her daydreams during the next hours were concentrated on what she would spend on dresses and accessories for herself and her little daughter, on fine furniture, delightful vacations, and so on. Besides, she could pay off some heavy debts incurred (without her husband's knowledge), and be rid of that burden easily. To her dismay, she found that the amount needed to satisfy all that she wished was far beyond what the life insurance money could provide.

This sobered her, but she was still not aware of the fact that the premise of her daydreams and speculations was the death of her husband. Only in the psychoanalytic sessions did she understand that this wish was the unconscious premise of all her plans and pleasurable anticipations. This case resembles that inferred in *"tuer son mandarin,"* not only with regard to the motive of money as profit, but also in so far as here, too, the person unconsciously has murder in mind.

But there are other consolations in the fantasies of young women who imagine themselves as widows —amorous consolations, and some gratifying to a harmless feminine vanity. When I was in Paris as a young man, I heard a ditty which was meant to console a young widow:

> *Ne pleure pas;*
> *Le noir te va si bien.*

> *Don't cry;*
> *Black is so becoming to you.*

The reader has observed that various discussions of neurotic disturbances reported by colleagues and students are presented here along with those from my own psychoanalytic practice. Such presentation shows not only the diversity and variety of unconscious death wishes, but also their emergence in almost all cases of neurosis. (Sometimes I even forgot to jot down the name of the colleague or student who reported the case.)

Here are a few cases from my own psychoanalytic practice. A man almost fifty-five years old, father of two children, once consulted me because he often felt, as he said, "a cloud in his mind," unable to think clearly and logically. Only a few psychotherapeutic sessions were necessary to find the source of that clouding. It always occurred when he thought of his rich father-in-law. The patient lived in straitened circumstances; he was a religious man, and did not admit to himself that he wished that his father-in-law would die and leave his daughter and the children a good portion of his money.

Let me contrast that example with one of a nineteen-year-old student who came from Cincinnati to attend New York University. He complained frequently about choking sensations for which, as his physicians declared, no organic cause could be found. The occasions in which he had such attacks were of a very different kind. In the initial interview he spoke of his relationship with his father and said, "I am quite fond of him. We try to understand each other"—and then, correcting himself, "or rather, to accept each other." (Psychoanalysts pay careful attention to such almost imperceptible messages.) In a relatively short time the young man had choking attacks at the following occasions: when he went to the theater, when he took a girl to a rather luxurious restaurant, and when he allowed himself a meal in a fancy French café. The thought associations accompanying his report left no doubt of the origin and nature of his choking sensations.

Each time he thought that his father, who was a very frugal man, would object to his extravagance and reproach him for his spendthrift living. The son would not defend himself, but he would wish the father would choke on his words. This wish turned against him in the sense of unconscious punishment, brought about those tormenting choking sensations.

Psychologically akin to this case is another in which a young man was called home when his father became dangerously ill. When Bill arrived, he found his father dying and for the first time felt "safe with him," as he said, because he knew his father would no longer ask why he was spending so much money in New York.

In most of those cases, the death wish is accompanied or followed by self-sabotage or self-punishment. The clouding of the mind and the choking sensations are transparent examples of such unconscious "moral" reaction. The presence and the efficiency of those factors operating in most cases of death wishes would be sufficient to reject Murray's sarcastic remarks about the Satanic role of psychologists. Were not psychologists the observers and the describers of those reactions? And did not psychologists recognize that it was unconscious love for those persons whom one had wished dead that was behind those reactions?

A more serious and an irresistible argument can be advanced against those critics; they are convinced that we act freely. More than this, they entertain the more dangerous illusion that we think and feel freely.

Some readers will, I am sure, remember the story of the old couple on their golden wedding day. Husband and wife were asked whether they had ever considered divorce during those fifty years. "Divorce, never," said the man; "murder, frequently."

Are such impulses avoidable when people live intimately

for many years? Hardly; let's face the music. We may not like the tune, but we have to dance to it.

Is it really so harmless when people take such delight in the rhyme about Lizzie Borden?

> *Lizzie Borden took an axe*
> *Gave her mother forty whacks;*
> *When she saw what she had done*
> *She gave her father forty-one.*

The Case of a Weak Memory

When airplane travel was still rare, the satirical writer Karl Kraus in Vienna once complained: "It would not be so far to Africa, but until you can come to the South Railway Station—that takes a very long time." It is similar with the approach to certain problems. Why did I need such a circuitous road to arrive at the core of the problem?

The case of that woman lawyer I treated more than twenty years ago would have led me more directly to the goal. Not all details of that case remain in my mind, but strangely enough, I fully recollect other, perhaps even less important features. I will remember, for instance our first interview. The woman had told me that she was working in the office of the prosecuting attorney and complained about certain defects of her memory in cross-examining a defendant. I was astonished to hear that she was with the attorney for the prosecution. I remember that initial surprise as well as my next thought associations, perhaps because I told them to the patient much later. Why should a woman who looked so feminine and was interested in various philanthropic enterprises choose such a job? It occurred to me that in ancient Rome, when a murderer was led to execution and succeeded in touching the garment of a priestess of Vesta, an old goddess, he was freed. Was this not symbolic of the task that women have on earth?—namely, to protect life rather than to destroy it?

The patient had various nervous symptoms, the most conspicuous of which was loss of memory when she had to cross-examine defendants and witnesses. At times she suddenly failed to recall certain important facts and could scarcely conceal her embarrassment. This aberration first appeared when she had the task of grilling an old Jew who had fraudulently declared bankruptcy, but it was not restricted to this case; soon it became generalized and appeared whenever she had to cross-examine people.

I succeeded in removing other neurotic symptoms, but I failed to conquer that irksome weakness or loss of memory which so disturbed the patient. At the end of her psychoanalytic treatment I could only advise her to choose some other area of the legal profession where she did not have to face such situations. As far as I know, she did so and has been successfully occupied in her new field.

Here are a few facts from her history. Her parents came to the United States from Russia or Poland as poor immigrants. Her father never learned to speak proper English, although her mother had higher aspirations. The patient remembered that in elementary school, she had a crush on a woman teacher. On one occasion, aware that her teacher was walking behind her, she turned toward a beautiful brown house in an effort to have the teacher believe that she lived there instead of in a miserable building in the slum section of New York.

Her father opened a little secondhand clothing store. He was often vulgar and rude, and made terrible rows with his wife and children over the least extravagance. He was stingy, and he never paid his debts punctually. However, he invariably and promptly paid his high premiums on his life insurance.

As an example of her father's stinginess the patient reported that, as a little girl, she once brought home a dog because the animal had followed her. When the dog had puppies, her father got rid of them because it cost too much to feed them.

As a child, the patient hated her father and not only on account of his miserliness and the rows, but also on account of his embarrassing crudeness.

Some weeks before she went to her first dance in high school, she asked her father for a new dress. He flatly refused. At the same time her younger brother wanted to go to a football game. The dollar he wanted from his father was indignantly denied.

Business was poor at the time. A competitor had opened a similar store across the street. The old man's temper did not improve because of it.

On the evening before the daughter's first dance something strange happened. The father called her into the store and asked her what she needed. She chose a dress, but he said, "Take another one," and "Don't you need also a fur jacket?" and made her take various items of clothing. The girl was surprised and taken aback. Father gave her brother two dollars and told him he could stay away until late.

When the girl came home at daybreak from her dance, the first thing she saw as she entered the apartment was her father's body hanging on the cross bar of the window. He had committed suicide.

Because he had always paid his life insurance premiums promptly, he left his family well provided. The girl and her brother could comfortably finish their studies with no worries about the future.

Let us now return to the symptoms of the patient, especially to the lapses of memory. (Since the patient is living I restrict the history to this single aspect.) That case of the old Jew and his fake bankruptcy must have reminded the patient of her father. This unconscious memory was the cause of her loss of memory with regard to data when she had to cross-examine the defendant. We know that this memory weakness or loss became generalized when the lawyer was put into the same situation. The conclusion is inevitable. That remarkable memory fault kept her from grilling that defendant and others for days afterward.

What was it that interfered so dramatically with her otherwise excellent memory? What was it that dulled her faculty of remembering? We can guess: It must have been her unconscious love for her father, perhaps awakened by the recollection of that scene prior to his suicide, and by other forgotten scenes in which the tough father played with and caressed the little girl. Psychoanalysis had revived those fragments of memory. It did more than cast light on the past that was almost unknown to her; it also paved the way to a better or more satisfactory life for the patient.

The Case of a Potential Mother

Most neurotic patients we treat suffer, as Freud once said, from unconscious reminiscences. They can be understood only historically and can prove the power of the past in the present.

Before I sketch the case of a potential mother, I would like to point out that unconscious death wishes of mothers against their children are by no means rare. A Dutch student of mine, a psychiatrist, Dr. A. Versteegh, showed that such wishes are frequently found in lullabies where you would least suspect their existence. Who would imagine them in the sweet songs mothers sing to put the baby to sleep? Yet they are present among all nations and in various forms, from the prediction that a bough will break to the threat that a tiger will devour the child. The situation in many cases prompts the emergence of such violent fantasies: The mother is very tired and wants the child to go to sleep, but the baby doesn't want to sleep yet and the mother loses patience.

Occasionally you even hear of a mother's death wish toward her unborn child. Françoise Mallet-Joris in a recent book speaks of the terror of childbirth.[43] (The child Vincent is now six years old.) She described the torment and "that shout that, to my astonishment, I heard come out of myself. Take it away and kill it."

At times women wish the embryo dead when they have a serious conflict with the child's father. I remember the case of a mother who became increasingly impatient with her two children until she finally shouted at them, "Go to the playground!" When the kids had gone, she experienced extreme fear that something terrible could happen to them—yes, that both of them might be killed on the way. She was compelled to run after them, and became calmer only when she saw them both safe. What appears as anxiety torturing the mother was originally the content of her unconscious violent wishes toward the children. It is not surprising that teachers who love children occasionally feel an upwelling of hostility toward them, especially when the children exhaust the teachers' patience. An excellent teacher whom I once treated, and who sometimes experienced such sudden feelings of hate, brought me a book written by a teacher, titled *Our Enemy, the Child.*

But perhaps the time has come to drop preliminaries and side remarks and to launch into a case history which requires some detail in telling.

A student of mine, Mrs. Gisela Tauber, who had been treating patients under my supervision, was concerned with a very intelligent woman of about thirty, a substitute teacher. This patient lived with her mother, with whom she was constantly quarreling. At times she screamed at her mother, "Drop dead!" When her analyst told her that these words expressed a death wish, the patient crossly denied this and said that it was just a way of speaking.

The case took on some exceptional features. This intelligent and well-educated teacher was promiscuous and yielded sexually to every man who wooed her. When Mrs. Tauber tried to convince her that promiscuous women have a low opinion of themselves as well as of their sex, the patient behaved better for a short time. However, she was often overcome by doubt and suffered a relapse as a consequence. She regretted whenever this happened, and once asked her analyst, "Should I have phoned you at one o'clock in the morning to get your opinion?"

The patient was unwilling to admit that she ever had death wishes toward her mother or others. When she again indignantly denied that she ever had such murderous thoughts, her attention was suddenly diverted to two points on the ceiling of the analyst's consulting room. She said that the two points gave her the impression of two eyes that looked disapprovingly at her. She recognized that they reminded her of the eyes of the analyst looking at her searchingly. On this unexpected detour about the transference the patient finally understood something of her emotional attitude toward her mother.

This teacher was in general inclined to deny the power of the emotional factors and liked purely intellectual discussions. As a teacher in elementary school, she never showed her annoyance or anger toward the children, although many of them were naughty or disobedient. Once she was surprised herself by her irrational behavior. During class, a little girl had taken out a small doll and began to fondle it. Without saying a word, the teacher went over to the child, took the doll, and threw it out the window.

Mrs. Tauber recalled something the teacher had mentioned casually but had never brought up again during the psychoanalytic treatment.

What were the reasons for the patient's irrational behavior and of her "acting out" in that scene? As a college girl she had had her first sexual experience with a professor who was the father of several children; she had become pregnant by him. Her mother would have condemned her bitterly if she had known of the pregnancy. An abortion had become necessary and this was done. The patient had once mentioned that experience, which had occurred ten years before the beginning of her treatment. Her irrational behavior toward that little girl in class presented an excellent occasion to return to that old, almost forgotten experience.

There was no doubt about what the scene meant unconsciously. Throwing the doll out so cruelly had the unconscious significance of getting rid of a child—one might say of an abortion. (Compare with this interpretation the previously mentioned childhood memory of Goethe, who, as a boy of almost four, threw plates and pots out of the window. It was a magical way to get rid of the newborn brother.)

The teacher's behavior is thus psychoanalytically considered a repetition of what she herself once experienced, transferred to the little girl and her doll. In the scene itself she played two roles, like an actress with two parts in a play. She is the cruel mother who compels the daughter to get rid of an illegitimate child by an abortion. At the same time she is identified with the little girl whose doll she threw out. Becoming pregnant was an expression of her rebellion against her mother, whereas the abortion presented the self-punishment for those rebellious feelings.

The first result of the return to the theme of abortion was a childhood memory of the patient. She remembered her mother who looked at her and her brother "with a Mona Lisa smile" when they were children. She experiences a vivid feeling of envy of her mother, who is proud and happy with her children (in contrast to herself who is childless). Other thought associations follow the same direction. There appears the question of what had happened to the doll she had thrown out the window, and how old her own child would now have been.

The mistake we all make is perhaps that we undervalue the traumatic effect a first abortion has on a girl. It is difficult for a man to imagine the emotions aroused by this experience. Only the dark fantasy of castration approaches the character of that experience.

Other Strange Cases

A psychoanalyst who read the preceding portions of this book complained that the examples presented are mostly about women. He expressed the wish to learn more about the psychology of murder in the mind of the male. Let us therefore deal with a few instances of this kind.

My colleague Adolf Woltman treated a young man, Bill, who had been a stutterer since the age of five. Dr. Woltman reports:

> His mother wanted to send him to kindergarten, but this was perceived by Bill as a severe sign of rejection. He was sure that his mother was dumping him at the school and would forget about him. From then on his stuttering became more and more pronounced.
>
> When Bill was ten years old his mother became ill with cancer. She was in and out of the hospital. Somehow this boy knew that mother would have to die soon.
>
> When Bill was fourteen years of age, he heard that a famous television personality had stuttered in his youth but had been able to overcome it. Bill was able to get the name and address of this person and asked for an appointment. He had hoped that speaking to this man would help him to overcome his own deficiency. After he had written the letter he developed doubts. He felt that such good luck was too much to hope for; he felt that this could not happen to him. In typical obsessive,

compulsive fashion he formulated the notion that if he were to see this person his mother would die. In order to keep his mother alive, he would have to turn down any appointment. As things developed, he received a letter from that man inviting him to his office.

Bill enjoyed the interview; and then his mother died two days later. Although Bill knew that his mother would die, he nevertheless felt that he had killed her, that instead of seeing the TV person he should have declined the appointment. In other words, in some magical way he felt that he could have saved mother. Now that he had seen the TV person and lost his mother, he thought that he had killed her.

It is easy to guess that the patient must have once blamed his mother for his stuttering. As a little boy, unconsciously he wished her dead, and his present reactions prove his severe guilt feelings. Not many people get away with thought murders.

I no longer know if it was an older psychoanalyst or a participant in one of our seminars who told us about the following case. A young man came into consultation suffering from a severe depression. During the ensuing psychoanalytic treatment the patient revealed that he felt guilty because he had been responsible for the death of a girl with whom he had been engaged to marry and whom he had loved. He and the girl had agreed to meet a few weeks before at a certain place outside New York. Each of them was to arrive in his own car. They discussed trifling things, but they soon got into a violent quarrel. The young man drove away furiously, without a parting kiss and without saying good-bye to the girl. An hour later he heard that the girl had been killed in a car accident.

His depression and his guilt feeling had, of course, some

psychological causes, not only in the mourning, but also in the possibility that the girl, disturbed by the quarrel with her fiancé, may have paid less attention to traffic. This negligence would at least be partly responsible for the accident.

The main cause for this guilt feeling must have been that during the quarrel some unconscious death wishes had emerged in him. Then, when she was then killed a short time afterward, it was as if some superhuman power had carried out a death sentence formulated in his mind.

Here again we have an emotional reaction originating in the belief in evil wishes. Is it not as if everybody were compelled in his thoughts to kill the person he loves?

Quite different is the case of a patient reported by a student of mine, Dr. Leonard Kingsley. It obviously takes all kinds of people to make a world of murder in the mind. This patient was a Jewish man of twenty, brought up in a religious home. He had never kissed a girl. His one romantic experience was that he had held hands with a girl for a few minutes.

When the patient studied at the Yeshiva University in Baltimore, he suddenly had the definite conviction that his father in New York had died. (His way of rationalizing the lack of a telegram was that his family had once kept it secret when his grandfather had died.)

He wrote to his father but got no answer. He telephoned, but was told that father was not at home. Finally a rabbi in Baltimore was able to reassure him and to allay his fears.

The sudden outbreak of anxiety was followed by a dream in which he saw his father dead. The dream would have been very puzzling if it had not been preceded by an increasing sexual excitement in the young man. The patient, who was painfully bashful with women, had made the acquaintance of a young girl who had behaved seductively toward him. During the next few days he often felt sexually excited and had many fantasies in which he desired that girl.

The thought of his father's death emerging so suddenly travels in an old groove. It revives the memory trace of father as the rival and disturber of the little boy's love life. The death wish toward the father behind the young man's anxiety results from unconscious memories of the Oedipus constellation. The sexual deprivation, acutely experienced, awakened the dormant hostility against the father as if he were blocking the road.

From the intensity of the anxiety when the possibility of the father's death occurred to him, one can determine the vehemence of the forbidden wishes as one can estimate the force of a thrown ball from the rebound.

Here are two cases showing that hostility may turn against the wife in the same degree of intensity. A patient of my colleague David B. Margolis returned home one evening and did not find his wife there. (She had gone out with some women friends and came back much later.) The husband became restless and called all the hospitals in the city, gave the name and description of his wife, and expected at any moment to hear that she was the victim of an accident. At the same time he told himself that it was all nonsense, but he could not help telephoning the hospitals. The content of his anxiety reveals, of course, the nature of prior evil wishes of which the person was largely quite unaware.

A case described by Mrs. Margaret Krafft shows a different character. A man in his thirties was married to a woman about ten years his senior. He unconsciously wished his wife away because he was attracted by a younger girl. Faced with this situation, made clear to him by his analyst, he indignantly denied the existence of such thoughts. Yet he says that he often practices rifle shooting and that he wishes especially to shoot an old female cat that often comes into his garden. It is not only the sequence of thought associations that speaks so eloquently here; there is the transparent displacement of his concealed wishes from his wife to the animal.

A psychoanalytic critic found fault with my examples in that they did not clearly show the connection of guilt feelings with the Oedipus situation.

Freud used to say that one should listen intently to one's own critical voice; to the critical voice of others with some attention. I thus welcomed that criticism but did not do anything about rectifying any omission. I behaved like the archaeologist Heinrich Schliemann, who paid little attention to the middle strata of his excavations in his eagerness to discover Homer's ancient Troy near Hissarlik, and hewed his way to the lowest level where he found the remains of the city. Like him, I was most eager to arrive at the bottom of the problem.

Yet there was an obstacle, namely, a wish to go over what I have written instead of getting over it. Thus, when I reread the earlier portion, I understood in retrospect that I had indeed neglected to show what an important part was played by the tendencies originating in the Oedipus situation. To correct that omission at least partially, a single example will be presented here. A Jewish patient in his early thirties is impotent with Jewish women and can have successful sexual intercourse only with German girls, preferably those with Nazi leanings.

This will remind the reader of the exogamy of the primitive Australian and African tribes whose members display a superstitious fear of having intercourse with women of their own group. My patient, it seemed, was reminded by Jewish women of his mother and sister and had to avoid them on account of this displaced incestuous taboo.

I conjectured from certain interpretations that the patient as a small boy had once witnessed sexual intercourse between his parents. The impressions of that primal scene had later led to a castration fear in the boy, especially with regard to his mother and sister, and in later generalization to women belonging to the mother or sister group.

The patient angrily denied this reconstruction and then spoke of his eye troubles, of specific, rather unpleasant eye sensations for which the ophthalmologist found no organic cause. The patient expressed fear of going blind.

No light was cast upon the origin of those obviously neurotic eye sensations until the patient told me a dream, in which he saw himself as a boy in his room, half asleep. His mother came into the room to tuck him in. She was wearing nothing but a very thin negligee. The dreamer lay prone, with eyes closed and face pressed into the pillow.

The interpretation of this dream started from the fact that the dream distortion often shows the opposite of the latent content of the dream. (For instance, women who dream that they are wearing a fine fur coat conceal the thought that they appear nude on a certain occasion.) The patient with eyes closed and face pressed to the pillow thus reveals the opposite: he is staring at his mother; he wants to see her genitals.

On this detour we arrive at the Oedipus situation again. I could remind the patient that the mythical king of Thebes after his incestuous crime has been discovered, is not castrated, but blinds himself. (Displacement from below to above.)

It is not possible to fill all the gaps left in this essay. Many of them are, of course, owing to the defectiveness of my knowledge. I shall, however, try to fill a few gaps and at least to diminish others. It is necessary, for instance, to point out that fleeting death wishes occur much oftener than recurring and lasting ones.

In contrast to this case, murderous wishes often emerge

from an atmosphere that is not fierce, irrational, nor full of misdirected hatreds. Such a fantasy may well surprise a person when he expresses his wish by saying, "It's time So-and-so was gathered to his fathers," or "If So-and-so were murdered it would be a boon to the nation." A person to whom such an idea occurs need not give it a second thought.

To give you a few instances:

A young man heard his girl friend, who had greatly annoyed him an hour before, singing, "June is busting out all over," from Richard Rodgers' musical. "Go bust yourself," thought the young man.

A woman who was present when a young girl flirted openly with her husband thought, "I could wring her neck."

In a first interview a young girl said that her aunt had told her that her parents' married life had been very unhappy. Father had often yelled at mother and had mercilessly criticized her. He had died when the patient was eleven years old. I asked her if she remembered if she was ever present at a quarrel between her parents. She answered, "No, but I was present at his death."

The answer seems evasive and is illogical, but it is psychologically fraught with meaning. It indirectly confirms my suspicion that she was sometimes present at her parents' quarrels in spite of her "no." It reveals, secondly, that the little girl took the part of the mother against father in those forgotten arguments. "But I was present at his death" seems not to fit the context, but it makes good sense when you interpolate the girl's thought: "I wish him dead because of his shouting at Mother, and he really died."

Fleeting violent wishes are frequent also during the psychoanalytic treatment. For instance, a patient felt most uncomfortable lying on the couch while I sat behind him, my legs stretched out on a footstool. He became more and more restless, and finally declared he was afraid that I would kick him in the head with my foot. This was, of course, a projection of his own unconscious violent feelings toward me.

This case is psychologically similar to that of a patient of Dr. Otto Fenichel.[44] This person was obsessively worried that the psychoanalyst would die during one of his sessions and was therefore compelled to turn around and look at the physician. Particularly, patients who strenuously resist the idea that they could once have had death wishes toward their father sometimes get a lasting impression from such transference fantasies.

Social climbers, in their fleeting daydreams, usually step over the bodies of certain people ahead of them in society. Such passing ideas were rarely taken seriously by the daydreamers themselves.

Some people get mad at somebody in the office or at home and think, "Go to hell!" and with that the anger blows over and that is the end of it. When they wish the boss or someone else dead, what's the harm? Sticks and stones can break bones, but fleeting fantasies concerning someone's death will not harm him.

I spoke in a previous section of my coronary attack following my second wife's death. I am sure I must have wished her dead during the many years she was in the nursing home, to a great extent because I had to work so hard to pay the bills. But it was shortly after she died that I was stricken. Thus it seems as if those thought crimes—I mean death wishes—demand severe self-punishment only when those wishes are fulfilled, when the fantasy turns into reality.

Theoretically, an emotionally healthy man could wish death to another human being without suffering much, as long as the wish fails. This may not sound pleasant to the ears of our moralists, but it is the truth. In this sense, everybody has a skeleton (or many) in his closet.

We have crossed the country in rapid excursions, from childhood fantasies to those of adults. Goethe put the following lines as a motto at the head of his collected poems: "Late resounds what early sounds." Perhaps the second line should be added: "Luck and ill to song are rounded." (*"Spät erkling was früh erklang, Glück und Unglück wird Gesang."*)

We would now like to understand the part that unconscious death fantasies played in the lives of two famous composers. Both men of genius, neither could escape those "natural shocks that flesh is heir to."

Gustav Mahler and Bruno Walter Consult Freud

The following pages present a partial analysis of the emotional attitude of Gustav Mahler to Hans von Bülow, the famous conductor of the Hamburg concerts. A good introduction to the subject would be to quote a letter of Alma Mahler, dated June 28, 1933. This letter of Mahler's widow to me was the answer to my inquiry about the relationship of Bülow to Mahler. I had visited Alma, who was then married to Franz Werfel, in Breitenstein on the Semmering. She, Franz Werfel, Victor Dirsztay, and I had spent a very nice afternoon and evening together.[45] We took a walk together and then had dinner in the beautiful cottage that Mahler had built in Breitenstein. I had wanted to ask her about Bülow and the composer, but it was scarcely the proper occasion, and I therefore postponed the question. This is her letter (originally in German).

Dear Dr. Reik: *June 28, 1933*

I remember you very well. You came with Dirsztay up to the Semmering. Mahler's attitude to Bülow was that of a disciple to his master. I was asked to accompany him to Bülow's coffin in the crematorium. Bülow had died in Egypt. During the Dies Irae the idea occurred to him [Mahler] for his Second Symphony. Instead of the "Great appell" the last movement should be called "Lux in tenebris lucet" (The light shines in the darkness). He thought that the people who, at the great kettledrum roll, are resurrected from the graves march past the Lord in troops that are without order and, before all, without class distinction. There is no guilt before the Lord. The birds' voices signify the receding. Otherwise all is music and therefore indefinable. Concerning that movement—so Mahler said—"It is as if you are lying on your back in a meadow, with the sky and the clouds above you, thinking of the person you love."

I shall not publish that second volume of the letters for the present.

Cordial regards,
Alma Mahler

This letter, written thirty-two years ago, is interesting in more ways than one.

I treated the development of the Second Symphony very fully in my book, *The Haunting Melody*[46] and I do not want to repeat myself, excepting some facts which it is necessary to recall. A very significant difference in Mahler's own conception of the symphony is in these facts. He explained to his friend, Natalie Bauer-Lechner, in January, 1896, that the symphony presents the life of a hero, his struggles, death, and redemption. Three months later he wrote Max

Marschall that a friend of the hero looks back on his life and death, and seeks its meaning.

This introduction of an observer marks not only a loosening of identification with that fallen hero but also the composer's growing independence from that figure. We know that Mahler at that time believed he would die early and that only then would his compositions be appreciated. "One need not be alive to become immortal," he said.

Mahler had greatly admired that master conductor von Bülow and asked him to accept him as a disciple. Very soon Bülow admired Mahler, who was thirty years younger, and recommended him later as his successor when he resigned.

There was, however, some discord in the relationship of the two men. Bülow admired Mahler as a conductor, but was horrified by his compositions. Mahler once played the *Totenfeier* for him (which was then conceived as an independent composition but later became the first movement of the Second Symphony). Bülow said at the time: "If this is music, then I don't understand music any longer." Mahler, in remarking upon this to a friend, said, "We separated quite amicably, nevertheless. . . ." How much is implied in that little word "nevertheless"!

Mahler was then thirty-one years old. When Bülow died in 1894 in Cairo, Mahler was only thirty-four and conducted the Hamburger concerts in Bülow's stead, which he had often done when the old master was indisposed.

Mahler had continued to compose the Second Symphony, but was unable to finish the last movement. In a letter to his friend Arthur Seidl, Mahler relates how the idea of the finale occurred to him:

"Bülow had just died and I attended the memorial service for him here. . . . At that moment, the choir near the organ intoned the Klopstock Chorale 'Resurrect'; it struck me like a bolt of lightning and everything stood clear and vivid before my soul . . . and yet, if I had not carried the idea with me, how could I have experienced it? There were a thousand people with me in the church at that moment."

Mahler is right; he must have had carried the idea a long time. Bülow had been ill for years and his death did not come as a surprise. When the boys intoned the choral of resurrection, the thoughts of the surviving Mahler were, of course, directed to the dead. But the verses

> *My wings that I have won, unfolding*
> *My fervent love outpouring,*
> *I shall be soaring,*
> *The light no eye has seen beholding. . . .*

are Mahler's. There appears the hope that his work, which Bülow had rejected, will live forever. The fear of death is conquered by the expectation of the immortality of the composer's work.

It must have been that Mahler's thoughts turned to that scene in which Bülow had so indignantly rejected the first movement of this very symphony.

During the scene with Bülow, an intense death wish toward the man who had so often been his benefactor, must have suddenly emerged and then was energetically suppressed.

Do we need any proof of the existence and the emotional consequences of this unconscious murderous impulse? I think not, but whoever doubts it will find proof enough in Mahler's letters. After Bülow's death his feelings toward the master are freely expressed. On the day of the cremation he writes: "At last the great day has come. We shall celebrate it from nine in the morning till around five o'clock." The ironical tone expresses only Mahler's impatience, but what is one to say about the rest of this letter? "My whole hope is that the mourning ladies will not now establish a Bülow museum (and perhaps exhibit the chamberpots and laundry slips). How people carry on about a dead Bülow, while letting the young and living ones toil and suffer."

Here certainly is a revival of those suppressed feelings brought to the surface on a detour, a return of emotions after they have been suppressed. Here finally is a kind of envy of the dead person and then an evident egotistical turn-in toward one's own person. There can be no doubt of this.

Thus we see an intensive murderous impulse toward a much admired person; its repression and its return from the emotional confinement of the netherworld; fear of retaliation in the form of one's own death; and finally conquest of this death fear and the certainty that one's work will win out.

I referred elsewhere in this book to the consultation Mahler had in Holland with Freud many years later. The crisis with which Mahler was confronted was of a different kind. However, there is no need to discuss it here.

Bruno Walter himself has described his first meeting with Mahler and his collaboration with Mahler in Hamburg.[47] Years later, Mahler invited him to conduct the Vienna Opera, which Walter accepted after being invited a second time. He tells us in his book that he, "a young man of twenty-two, felt my own powers growing and my independence developing . . . and I had hesitated to place myself then under the guidance of Mahler and—a thought which had not occurred to me—to run the risk of jeopardizing my own self-development." In the fall of 1901, Bruno Walter first appeared as conductor of the Opera. The friendship deepened between him and Mahler. Walter was not feeling well in Vienna later, but he stayed there. He was present at the

Grinzing cemetery when Mahler was buried on May 18, 1911.

Walter remained eleven years in Vienna. In his autobiography, *Theme and Variation*, he described how he was visited by a mysterious complaint. Even the wording of that report is significant; ". . . the guardian angel to whom my education and chastisement were entrusted had felt it proper" . . . "to give me an illness that caused me great anxiety." It was a pain in the arm, and it was especially excruciating when he used his right arm for conducting. When all the physicians he consulted asserted that there was an important psychogenic factor in the ailment, and when a number of treatments did not help, Walter consulted Freud,[48] and was resigned to "submit to months of soul-searching." The consultation had an unexpected character.

Freud examined his arm briefly and attentively listened to Walter's story. Instead of getting involved in the patient's childhood experiences, Freud asked if he had ever been to Sicily. He advised Walter to leave immediately, forget all about his arm and the Opera, and journey off to Sicily. Walter did as he was told. He tried not to think of his malady, but instead used his eyes.

When Walter returned after some weeks in which he had been greatly impressed by Hellenism, he went to Freud, who advised him to resume his work as a conductor. But Walter complained that he could not move his arm. Freud said, "Try it at any rate!" and declared that he would take the responsibility.

Thus Walter again began to conduct. At the next session with Freud, the analyst again attributed particular importance to forgetting the ailment. Walter, it seems, said that he sometimes forgot his arm during the music. Thus, "by dint of much effort and confidence, by learning and forgetting," as Walter says, he succeeded finally. He was able once more to conduct.

Why did Freud adopt this strange technique in this particular case?

At first it looks very much as if he were being entirely paradoxical and arbitrary. There is at the outset his advice to forget all about conducting and the Opera and to look at the beauty of Sicily, then the advice to conduct and forget all about the arm. But to begin with, what was the nature of the arm ailment? According to Walter, some physicians called it a "professional cramp," but he adds, "It looked deucedly like incipient paralysis." The doctors all agreed that there were psychogenic factors in the ailment.

We know now what it was. It was hysteria, and the arm pain had the character of a conversion symptom, which means "changes of physical functions occur, which unconsciously and in a distorted form give expression to instinctual impulses that previously had been repressed. Hysterical paralysis is, like all "motor paralysis, a defense against action," as Freud declares. . . . Hysterical paralysis shows, says Freud, an exact delimitation and an extreme intensity, "and the lesion associated with it is independent of the anatomy of the nervous system," since hysteria induces paralysis and other manifestations, as if the anatomy were nonexistent, or as if it had no knowledge of it." [49]

Freud had made a special study of the difference between organic and hysterical paralysis, and he must have recognized, after the examination of Walter's arm and after listening to his story, that the complaint had all the earmarks of a hysterical symptom.

But why didn't Freud treat Walter according to psychoanalytic methods, and why did he advise him to forget conducting and opera and run off on a Sicilian tour? We don't know, but we can guess the reasons. The paralysis appeared especially while Walter was conducting, and we can conclude that there was a particular resistance against this activity on whose perfection Bruno Walter worked with all his energy. Where is the origin of this resistance to a task the young conductor loved? The answer is: He did not want to be a conductor under Mahler or with him. Unconsciously he wanted to be the only conductor of the opera and of the philharmonic concerts. We remember that he reluctantly accepted Mahler's invitation to become his co-conductor, and that he doubted at first that he could maintain his independence from Mahler. Freud recognized the character of the paralysis as a defense (against the wish to remove Mahler and succeed to the envied position).

If it were necessary to strengthen the validity of this hypothesis, I would quote Walter's own words. "As long as Mahler was active in the opera, my position and that of my colleague, Franz Schalk, were overshadowed by his." [50] Here the bitterness Walter felt is expressed in this hidden form.

The painful arm symptom also had the character of unconscious self-punishment for the evil wishes against Mahler, toward whom Walter had an ambivalent attitude. Freud hoped that an interruption of the conducting activity and of the thoughts focused on Mahler and the opera would help Walter overcome his moral scruples and self-destructive tendencies, and to enable him to continue his work without punishing himself for his murderous thoughts.

Walter was soon invited to give concerts in other cities, and the Mahler episode drew to a close when the composer went to America and said a final good-bye to the Vienna Opera.

The old play had repeated itself: the death wish, Mahler's toward von Bülow, had been fulfilled, just like the unconscious Walter's wish to remove Mahler and to supplant him was fulfilled in some form. Both men could not bear to remain in the sphere of music in the position of second fiddle. Walter conducted the first performance of Mahler's *Song of the Earth* after the composer's death.

A Rumanian proverb says: "Behind every ball there is a child in pursuit of it." In the same way, is there not a race for glory and social position in men, who are all grown-up boys? The Roman goddess Fortuna was usually portrayed as standing on a rolling ball.

Marginal Remarks on the Belief in the Evil Eye

Recent scientific literature on homicide reveals some interesting additions to our psychological knowledge. Walter Bromberg's book, for instance, discusses the relative infrequency of criminal offenses among women compared with men.[51]

There are, however, only a few books and papers dealing with the superstitious belief in the omnipotence of evil wishes. It seems that belief, once so widespread, has become obsolete and is now restricted to obsessional patients and to very ignorant people. Some forms of superstition survive in Italy and Spain; for instance, the belief in the evil eye.[52] An informative magazine article recently presented abundant material regarding the survival of that superstition among certain levels of the Italian population.[53]

We should not be astonished about the conception of the eye as a deadly weapon. Do we not speak of "shooting glances" at someone, and of "murderous glances." Oscar Wilde said:[54]

> *Yet each man kills the thing he loves,*
> *By each let this be heard,*
> *Some do it with a bitter look,*
> *Some with a flattering word,*
> *The coward does it with a kiss,*
> *The brave man with a sword!*

We purposely restrict ourselves to the area of Italy, Sicily in particular. To present only a few significant examples from those countries, in which the belief that "there are malevolent *jettatore* around." The Pope Pius IX and Monsignor Prosperi were widely believed to be *jettatore*. A few months after his election (in 1846) the Pope was driving through the streets of Rome and happened to glance at a window where a nurse was holding a child. The child fell from her hands and was killed. On the day he blessed the column erected to the Virgin in the Piazza di Spagna, a worker fell from the scaffold to his death. Pius IX's successor, Pope Leo XIII, was also said to have the evil eye. The murder of King Humbert in 1900 was attributed to the *jettatura* of Leo XIII.

To give another typical example of this belief, taken from the same magazine article, a Neapolitan woman had the evil eye without knowing it. A friend who found her husband chatting with this woman wanted to protect him and casually slipped her arm around his neck, as a *corno*, or shield. She forgot that she was wearing a poisonous ring. It scratched his neck and he died in a few minutes.

It is important to differentiate between the voluntary and involuntary possessors of the evil eye. Byron, Napoleon II, Wilhelm II, the composer Jacques Offenbach, and many others were, according to popular belief, *jettatore*. A story is told of Professor Rodolfo Fanciani, a professor at the University of Rome, who once entered a café in Naples. He took a table not far from the chandelier. It fell, killing several persons.

King Alfonso XIII of Spain was also believed to be a *jettatore*. He visited Italy in 1923. When he stepped ashore in Naples, a saluting gun exploded and killed its entire crew. An officer who belonged to the reception committee shook hands with King Alfonso, and immediately afterward threw a fit and died.

Enough of these examples. I only want to illustrate how murderous wishes, operating by means of the evil eye, are still in the realm of belief. This opens up the wide field of black magic and witchcraft, so we had better break off the discussion of forbidden tendencies at work in those extensive superstitions. Let us also resist the temptation to speak of certain forms of homicide that are strange variations, such as "psychic homicide," the subject of an article by J. A. Merloo.[55] (By the way, why hasn't anyone, as far as I know, discussed "killing with kindness"?)

Just a few side comments on some peculiar American phrases: a person will sometimes introduce a joke with the words, "This one will kill you," meaning that it will overwhelm you. (Compare the German expression: "*Das ist zum Totlachen.*") We also say, "He made a killing in the stock market," meaning a sudden financial success. We speak of a "killing frost," and of a "kill-joy," and of an "hour to kill." We say also, "She is dressed to kill," meaning she is dressed in such a way that no man can resist her. Thus we reveal that we are aware of our human weakness and defenselessness. We assert in vain that we are just "killing time." In the end, time will kill us.

All these expressions are, of course, gross exaggerations.

It is undeniable, however, that such phrases reveal the trace of some violence—we might almost say a sadistic trend.

The Murderous Wishes of Groups

Newspapers reported a strange occurrence in Albany not long ago. A young man stood for a long time on the ledge of a high building, declaring that he was going to jump to his death. Nothing new about this story, but there was something particularly absurd about the crowd's behavior in the street below. People were shouting up to the boy. Some yelled, "Jump!" or "Come on, you coward!" or "Are you yellow?" and in similar phrases goaded him to carry out his threat. A woman became impatient and regretfully said that if the man did not jump soon she would have to go home to feed her children. Is this not nauseatingly horrible?

How can we explain such behavior in a crowd—certainly contrasting with the attitude of the individual? Can it be a kind of emotional "drain" reaction? We know from Freud's penetrating inquiry into the group psychology[56] that such a difference exists. Freud, who frequently refers to G. Le Bon's splendid characterization in his *Psychologie des Foules*,[57] stated that the repression operating in the individual is released in the group, and that the unconscious, wherein all the evil in the human soul is present, takes supreme command. Conscience and feeling of responsibility vanish. Groups do not tolerate delay, and their emotions are always extreme. A person who is perhaps an educated man becomes, in a crowd, a bestial barbarian, governed solely by violent impulse.

There are other cases in which the concealed death wishes in the groups re-emerge and are freely and uninhibitedly expressed. A physician asserted that people attending death-defying stunts at circuses and the like, while they are "apparently shuddering in horror at the dangers, they are in reality fascinated and attracted by the possibility of instant death and really want to see an accident happen." [58]

The descendants of those who demanded that all aristocrats be hanged (*"à la laterne"*) during the French Revolution behaved quite similarly two hundred years later during the recent Algerian crisis. The young Frenchmen shouted, "To the cemetery with the oldsters." (*"À la tombe les ancêtres!"*) The "young Turks" always turn rebelliously against the conservative and reactionary old generation.

Crimes otherwise detested and loathed by the individual are unhesitatingly and deliberately committed when the individual is driven by the political fanaticism of the group. Princes and presidents are murdered without consideration of the far-reaching and catastrophic consequences of the crime. The murder of Archduke Franz Ferdinand led to the First World War, and no one can tell what the reactions will be to the assassination of President Kennedy.

Besides, it is not unusual that the political assassin does not feel guilty. He may think of the murder he committed as the good deed of the day. And why? Is it vain to ask oneself: "Could I have contributed in any way to the prevention of such a tragedy? Can the individual influence the psychological climate in a decisive manner?" [59]

Such questions posed by a psychiatrist after the assassination of President Kennedy seem to imply that the emotion of groups or crowds are merely negative. Yet it is only fair to state that they are sometimes as earnest and enthusiastic as those of the individual man and woman. Just the memory of John Kennedy's assassination shows us that crowds also know depression, discouragement, and mourning. We still remember the initial shock we all felt; we could not believe that such a crime was possible. We can still vividly recall the horror and overwhelming indignation shared by all ranks of society. Almost everybody unconsciously identified the young President with an older brother or friend.

It was, of course, the special personality of John F. Kennedy that accounts for the depth of mourning. I remember that the assassination of Archduke Franz Ferdinand did not awaken such reactions among all the people of Austria.

A survey conducted by psychiatrists and psychoanalysts revealed that those patients who showed no emotional reactions upon the President's death were mentally and emotionally the most serious cases.

The preceding considerations make us aware of the significance of the leader for the psychology of groups and collectives.

G. Le Bon's otherwise excellent characterization of group psychology does not consider the important role of the leader. Freud highly evaluates that role: all members of a group identify themselves with the leader and feel loved by him while he loves none of them. Yet he is sure of their approval and their applause and even of their enthusiasm for him. This encourages him to express murderous wishes freely against political enemies within his dominion and against the enemy outside, as for instance against other nations or groups of another social system.

In this collective position, death wishes carefully repressed or concealed in the individual will become conscious and are uttered impassionately. Khrushchev could thus violently threaten the American people: "We will bury you!" and

Nasser predicted that he and the Egyptian army will drown the Israeli in the sea by Passover of 1966. Sure of the approval of their people, these leaders express their murderous plans, just as children sure of their parents' approval will openly threaten other children.

Dionysius, the tyrant of Syracuse, invited Damocles to share the luxury he so much envied. At the banquet, a sword hung suspended over Damocles' head by a single hair. Thus he was to be reminded how precarious were the joys of luxury and glory. The sword of Damocles in our own time is the H-bomb, which has since Hiroshima been a threat over our heads. A holocaust beyond imagination can be brought about by the malevolent finger of a single man.

One need not be an uncritical follower of Arnold Toynbee in agreeing with him that only one choice exists: "One world or no world." [60] The accusations of Chinese and Russian Communists has reached new peaks in verbal ferocity. Here are open death wishes of one society against another. The world situation is under the shadow of an apocalypse and of a third world war that would set in motion and actualize every repressed murderous tendency. No Goya can present the "Horrors of War" in this nuclear age. They transcend human imagination.

I must add as a supplement to previous remarks that in war, also, impulses otherwise forbidden are expressed because a kind of "war superego" is created, a kind of superficial and passing identification, that Freud called the "parasitic double of the superego." [61] This "war superego" not only permits, but even demands, that murderous tendencies are brought into action.

Plato said: "Only the dead have seen the end of war."
How did Freud see that problem?

Freud and the Future

How did Freud see that problem? I asked myself again next morning, but there was no immediate answer. I see images first, then ideas, when I awake early in the morning. Thus it was on this occasion. I saw myself as a young psychoanalyst, perhaps at the age of twenty-six, waiting at a certain place on the Ringstrasse. This happened frequently.

After dinner Freud regularly took a long walk, always along the same route—from the Berggasse, where he lived, to the Ringstrasse, and then to the Kaerntnerstrasse, and then by way of a place called the Freyung home. So often I counted on meeting him at some point where I accompanied him home, discussing some problem in psychoanalytic practice and theory.

I see in my mind's eye again the Kaerntnerstrasse, a kind of promenade, where early in the evening well-dressed men and women strolled, and at night even better-dressed ladies awaited prospective clients.

Freud, who walked rather fast, followed this route while mulling over the subjects he meant to write about when he reached home.

I was at the Kaerntnerstrasse a few years ago, on a visit to my native town after an absence of many decades. How different the street appeared to me! Yes . . . other days, other ways.

I recalled what the Kaerntnerstrasse looked like on New

Year's Eve, one of the few evenings when Freud did not follow his regular route and daily routine.

The Vienna Opera had always on New Year's Eve a gala performance of *Die Fledermaus*. This most tuneful of all operettas, filled with *joie de vivre*, is climaxed by the great scene in the second act, presenting the party at Prince Orlovsky's. The ladies and gentlemen, after the performance, used to promenade on New Year's Eve on the Kaerntnerstrasse, singing the wonderful tune that was sung at that Orlovsky ball:

> *Brüderlein, Brüderlein und Schwesterlein*
> *Wollen wir alle sein,*
> *Stimmt mit ein.*
> *Brüderlein, Brüderlein und Schwesterlein,*
> *Lasst das traute Du uns schenken*
> *Für die Ewigkeit*
> *Immer so wie heut*
> *Wenn wir morgen noch dran denken*
> *Erst ein Kuss, dann ein Du*
> *Du, Du, immerzu. . . .*

It is a pity that there is no good translation for those stanzas. It would also be difficult because it would presuppose a good knowledge of Viennese habits and customs. In Vienna people call each other "*Sie*" (you) as elsewhere. Only near relatives, friends and lovers call each other "*Du*" (comparable to the archaic English "thou"). When two people want to be on very intimate terms they "drink brotherhood," which means they toast each other over a glass of wine, kiss, and call each other "*Du*" henceforth. The kiss is part of the ceremony, and goes with the drinking of wine. That allusion (*Erst ein Kuss, dann ein Du*) of course gets lost in the translation.

> *Brothers, brothers and sisters*
> *We all want to be,*
> *Join in with me*
> *Brothers, dear brothers and sisters,*
> *Let's get on intimate terms, let's be closest friends*
> *For all eternity,*
> *Just exactly as we are tonight.*
> *When we think of it still tomorrow*
> *Let's call one another "thou"—*
> *First a kiss, then a "thou"*
> *"Thou, thou, thou."*

(I use the translation from the gala performance of *Die Fledermaus* conducted by Herbert von Karajan.)[62]

In my youth I was often on the Kaerntnerstrasse and shared that Viennese form of Bacchanalia, drawn to it by the general gaiety and fun. When the midnight bells of St. Stephen's Cathedral sounded, people wished each other a Happy New Year, but most of them sang *"Brüderlein, Brüderlein und Schwesterlein, / Wollen wir alle sein."*

But I am lost in reminiscences and I wanted to speak of Freud. Living in Vienna most of his life, he understood the Viennese. He knew they all liked to be liked and were ready to offer all kinds of sacrifices for this—most readily, perhaps, even their convictions. Freud had, throughout his life, an ambivalent attitude toward Vienna. He well knew what that easygoing *"Brüderlein und Schwesterlein"* meant, and how hypocritical and deceitful it was. I often heard him make disparaging remarks about the Viennese.

I hope I shall not be considered a local patriot when I add that the Viennese themselves are well aware of their character. Indeed, doesn't the song itself show it? Doesn't it vow eternal brotherhood, qualifying the promise "when we think of it still tomorrow"? In this self-irony there is a conciliatory feature.

Emerging from the flood of reveries and reminiscences, I am trying to return to my original question: What did Freud think of those immense problems, of war and peace, and of the future of mankind? I take the last volume of his collected papers from the bookcase.

At the conclusion of his book *Civilization and Its Discontents* he says that "the question of destiny for human species seems to be whether and to what extent the cultural development will succeed in conquering the disturbance of living together created by instinctual aggression and self-destruction."

Man has advanced so far toward the control of natural forces that nations are capable of destroying each other to the last man. Therefore the present anxiety. One would expect that now the other heavenly power, the eternal "Eros" (the love of mankind) will make "a mighty effort to assert itself in the struggle with its immortal adversary." But he adds, "Who can foresee the success and the outcome?" These words, which display a cautious, optimistic attitude, were written in 1929.

Three years later, in a correspondence with Albert Einstein, Freud discussed the question "Why war?" [63] Einstein had formulated certain questions about whether and how wars could be prevented. "Here are problems which only the psychologist can illuminate." Freud replied in a long letter which, together with Einstein's, was published by the Institut International de Cooperation Intellectuelle in Paris.

In closing, Freud's letter deals with the process of cultural development. This organic process, comparable perhaps to the domestication of certain species of animals, brings about emotional and mental changes, such as the strengthening of the intellect and the turning aside of aggressive tendencies. Under the influence of those factors not only an intellectual and emotional rejection of war develops "in us pacifists," but also "a constitutional intolerance."

One cannot say how long we may have to wait until all are pacifists, but it is perhaps not a utopian hope that the influence of cultural attitudes and of the justifiable fear of the effects of a future war will ere long end the pursuit of war. Freud adds: "By what means or roundabout ways, we cannot guess." Since this was said, more than thirty-two years have passed—not a long time in the course of civilization. We are still anxiously waiting or fervently hoping.

The Last Fragment of a Confession

Life is a interlocking jigsaw puzzle. When you insert the last and the next to the last piece within the frame, the whole picture which you see makes little sense. A skeptic will doubt that human life has more significance than that of the bees or ants, which have an even busier existence.

This is being written a few weeks after my seventy-sixth birthday. The Eastern Psychological Association and my own organization, the National Psychological Association for Psychoanalysis, devoted a whole forenoon in Philadelphia to a symposium they called "In the Tradition of Theodor Reik." The speakers, Milton Gurewitz, Jule Nydes, John Gustin, and Murray Sherman evaluated me as a writer and as a psychoanalyst, a searcher and reseacher, and so on.

Sitting on the dais with them and being seen by many psychologists and psychiatrists, I became absurdly self-conscious. I must have made a ludicrous impression.

Urged to make some comments, I got up and first of all, expressed my satisfaction in seeing many women in the audience, not only on account of the aesthetic pleasure, but also in the hope that the impression of the speeches we had heard would be reduced to its proper moderation. Women are realists and see things as they are and not as they may appear to people with a favorable bias. What would women say to the comment of one of the speakers who compared me to Freud? It must sound to them as it did to me, like comparing a mountain in the Catskills with Mt. Everest. I have always known the limits of my talent, which are restricted to some original observations and to the ability to write about them. Freud, however, was a genius. A critic justly called his writings a work that shook the world.

A speaker had remarked that Freud spoke of me, as Ernest Jones mentions in his biography, as "one of our best hopes." That was during the time of my early psychoanalytic books. It saddens me now that I have disappointed those early hopes.

The symposium in Philadelphia took place some months ago. Since then my students gave me a birthday banquet at the Americana Hotel in New York. It was in May, and as I sat with my family at a separate table and listened to the speeches and to the music, I had the sudden impression of living in a different age. I listened to the jazz which I neither understood nor liked, and watched the dancing of the young people without comprehending how they could enjoy it. Ah, the waltzes of my youth in Vienna!

All that is now past and I am sitting at my desk and would like to finish this little book. Above my desk are pictures of Freud. They also cover the wall opposite. I believe there are more than fifty of them; a friend called them manifestations of my hero worship.

I get up from my chair and begin to pace the room and the small anteroom. There are pictures of Anatole France, of Mahler, of Arthur Schnitzler, of Richard Beer-Hofmann— all men I had known and admired when I was young, all now dead these many years. I feel lonely. I look at the framed poem "The Lonely Road," by Beer-Hofmann and mechanically read the inscription: "For Theodor Reik, in remembrance of days gone by, cordially, Richard Beer-Hofmann. Wien. 4. I. 1935." I tried to translate the second stanza into English:

> _Every joy and every sorrow_
> _Pales to a dim reflection._
> _What once was bliss, once was terror_
> _Goes—leaves us with ourselves alone._

I return to the pictures of Freud. He was my great benefactor, my greatest teacher and adviser. There was no man except my father whom I loved more. And yet. . . .

My memories go back to the first time I saw Freud and to the many times thereafter when I climbed the stairs of Berggasse 19 to visit him. I often had heart palpitations like a girl on a date. I looked forward to a wonderfully stimulating conversation in which I was sure to learn so much. I remember the time when he suggested that I ought to study psychoanalysis. Every month he gave me a certain amount from his own pocket. He did this for many months and even continued doing so after I was married. (What older psychoanalyst would do the like today in America?)

He not only supported me but also helped me in so many

difficult situations. There was no man toward whom I felt such gratitude as to Freud. And yet. . . .

I remember the last time I saw him, when I flew from Amsterdam to Vienna. I spoke of this occasion at the end of my book *Listening with the Third Ear*.[64]

When the Nazis occupied Vienna, I was naturally increasingly anxious about Freud. I asked my sister, who still remained in Vienna, to see him and to ask him whether I could do anything to get him out of Austria. He reassured her, but my anxiety disturbed me more and more, and yet. . . . I do not search my conscience. I just wonder at myself.

When he arrived in London in 1938, I knew that he was safe at last. And then suddenly questions—no, wishes emerged in me. Will he not die soon? He was eighty-two then; I was fifty.

To tell the horrible truth, I was impatient for the news of his death. He should, I felt, make way for me; yet I knew that I could never take his place.

There is no use concealing that most painful bit of truth.

I have passed my seventy-sixth year, and this is the last fragment of a mortifying confession. I have had my day and it has been a long time. I have done my best, although in retrospect it was not very good. (I even felt flattered when a psychiatrist recently called me a "has-been"!)

Now, when I sit amid the circle of my students in a seminar discussing cases and the technical and psychological difficulties of psychoanalytic practice and theory, I frequently have an odd experience. I seem to catch the glance of one of those young men and I suddenly recognize that he wishes me dead and wants to take my place. Does he not know it? Is he aware of it?

"Therefore send not to find for whom the bell tolls; it tolls for thee."

Conclusion

This essay draws to its close. Let me freely confess that I considered it in my daydreams not only as a psychological study, but also as a thought-provoking *document humain*.

The reader and I have traveled a long way and so it is possible we scarcely remember any longer our point of departure, now that we are so near to our point of arrival.

The title *Murder in Mind* reminds us, because it means murder committed in fantasy, of what the Germans would call *Gedankenmord*. Here, another thought interferes with the continuation of my idea about my contribution. Orville Prescott recently remarked that although there's hardly a subject that hasn't been the theme of a novel, two subjects interest novelists more than others. One is sex and love with its delights and disasters, and the second is adolescence with its agony.[65]

The critic explains the preference for those two subjects by the limitations to which the experience of novelists are subjected. They know little about politics, business and science, but they have been young and they have been in love.

But is the view presented here not objectively too limited even for the emotional and mental life of people? Is not the soul, according to Schnitzler's expression "a wide country"? Is there no room for other problems besides those of sex, love, and adolescence?

Let us consider only the emergence of violent and murderous impulses. Is this not an experience everybody has had, whether he acknowledges or denies it? Like the rest of us, novelists also must have encountered temptations of this kind. There are other fantasies dreamed and effaced, conjured up and disappearing, but let us here restrict ourselves to this one subject.

The realm of fantasy is a free country, perhaps the only one left in the foreseeable future. In this area the mystery stories of the future may lose the character of the whodunit and acquire rather that of who wanted it. Dostoevsky was a pioneer in this direction when he wrote *The Brothers Karamazov* eighty-five years ago. I do not know a modern mystery writer who follows in his footsteps.

We spoke of Dostoevsky and this novel when we mentioned Freud's paper. This perhaps is the appropriate place to append a few remarks. Freud considers only the part of parricide in Dostoevsky's life and work. In reality the situation was far more complicated. This man Fyodor Mikhailovich Dostoevsky conceived, I am sure, many ardent murderous wishes. He must have wished his brother Michael dead (he died in 1864), and then his brother's family— which he felt obliged to support. Dostoevsky must have wished for the death of his first wife, Marie Isaewa, with whom he was not happy, especially since he had a passionate sexual affair with Paulina Suslova before his wife died. That man had the imagination of a mass murderer and *The Brothers Karamazov* reveals only a small part of his fantasies.

In the slow motion of retrospect we now remember what had been the point of our departure. It was that phrase *"tuer son mandarin."* It was assumed that there is a penniless young student in Paris to whom a mandarin in Peking would leave a fortune after his death. The question was: If that young man by an act of will could kill the mandarin thousands of miles away, without ever being discovered, would you consider the life of the mandarin safe?

We no longer believe in the power of thought and we are therefore not eager to grapple with that problem. Another question interests us more: Is it possible that the rich old man in Peking will not become the object of murderous wishes of the young student in Paris? Can he escape the evil fantasy of his presumptive heir? I do not believe it. As far as that goes, I think the mandarin doesn't have a Chinaman's chance.

Lake Placid
August, 1964

THREE
THREE

THE UNREACHABLES
*The Repetition Compulsion
in Jewish History*

The Compulsion to Repeat

Introduction

The title and subtitle of this essay require a preliminary remark. Not far from a New Hampshire town where I spent a summer vacation a few years ago, a Catholic priest delivered a sermon titled, "The Unreachables." This is what he called the Jews, whose history he discoursed upon eloquently. I did not hear the sermon, but I was told that he did not treat his subject in an anti-Semitic manner, but rather in a conciliatory manner. He stated simply that the majority of the Jews could not be converted to Christianity because they could not be reached.

As its subtitle announces, this essay also deals with a certain aspect of Jewish history, namely, with a definite recurring pattern in their fate, a pattern whose deeper significance has not yet been recognized by historians. If the spirit of Jewish history could speak, it would perhaps say, "No one knows the trouble I have seen—not even the Jews."

In a recent article Alfred Kazin pointed out that very few Jews know a great deal about their own history, even of modern times.[1] Kazin quotes a Yiddish writer who said of a student of the Torah that he "has roamed as far and as wide as an ancient who has outlived the years of Methuselah! He has been in Mesopotamia, in Canaan, in Egypt, in Persia and Medea, in Susa its capital, and in countless other lands as far as India and Cathay; also the wilderness and the desert has he frequented, and there he has hearkened to many marvelous things . . . of a sort which to all other people are an incomprehensible mystery; but among Jews it is a common everyday event."

But Kazin arrives at the conclusion that this student, who knows so much about the sacred history of the Hebrews, knows almost nothing about their mundane history.

Otherwise this book requires no preface because, as Charles Lamb said of his essays, it is itself all preface. It is a preface to a future exploration of a world-historic subject.

Hegel once remarked that history teaches "that people and government never have learned anything from history, or acted on principles deduced from it." [2] This is certainly correct, but is learning from it one of the prime "uses" of history? Mankind has never learned from it, but individuals —in this case the historians—have. They have often used and abused history to fashion a framework for their theories.

There are in history, as in physics and chemistry, certain problems which fascinate the experts, that is, which hold them spellbound, as if in the grip of terror. The researchers seem to hope that if they look away for a long time these questions will vanish, disappear like a strange delusion.

There is still another way to cope with a problem of this kind, namely, to focus the mind on its surface, to concentrate attention on the outside and on the details of the phenomenon. Such tactics are especially successful when the surface itself is interesting. The suspicion that something is going on backstage is easily put aside when the action on stage diverts the attention.

I should like to pose such a question, a question of a very definite kind, concerning the character of Jewish history. It is perhaps best to call this specific aspect *"die*

Wiederkehr des Gleichen" (the return of the same), to borrow an expression from Nietzsche. Let me state in these initial remarks that I do not mean that certain events occur, but that they occur again and again. Why is it that a clearly definite and definable sequence of events takes place in the history of this people, from prehistoric times until our own day? First of all, is it true that such a similar sequence of conditions existed and still exists? Is there a law at work, as in nature, like the periodicity of ebb and tide, or the metamorphosis from cocoon to butterfly?

Priority is not among the aims of this essay. It has been said that every intelligent thought has already been thought before (one might add the same of every stupid or silly idea). I have devoted quite a few years to the perusal of the pertinent (and often impertinent) literature on the subject. But nowhere have I found the kind of observations which are set forth here. This does not mean, of course, that they do not exist.

I have tried to catch the leitmotifs of the Jewish symphony, but can I assert that I succeeded in this endeavor? I can only say that I have listened to the music with rapt attention—sometimes with the third ear. I shall not try to describe the character of this symphony. The famous Austrian playwright, Franz Grillparzer, who had just read a book on Handel, was asked by a friend how he liked it. "It's not bad," he answered, adding, "but you know, described music is just like a dinner about which you hear full details." I merely want to define the nature of those leitmotifs.

Before I enter the realm of this search and research, I would like to remark at the outset that I shall try to present the problems in the simplest terms and to avoid embroidering upon them. I am not concerned here with their poetic or with their beautiful aspects. Einstein once wrote: "If you are out to describe the truth, leave elegance to the tailor."

Whether I succeed or fail in this effort, I am convinced that there is a concealed law operating in the structure and in the content of Jewish history. This law exists. It has only to be found—and it will be found. This is not only a problem of the past but also of the present. Not only a problem of yesterday or today, but also of tomorrow.

A New Approach

We start our exploratory tour from a seemingly distant point of departure: from a revealing result of individual psychoanalytic experience.

Most of those interested in psychoanalysis are inclined to consider Freud's early explanations of human behavior as original and startling. They often do not see how revolutionary and clarifying are the psychological contributions of Freud in his old age.

At the threshold of advanced age, Freud, then sixty-four years old, published his book *Beyond the Pleasure Principle* which advances a new theory on the nature of the drives.[3] At this point, let us leave out of consideration all biological and physiological ideas contained in that highly compressed work, restricting ourselves to a survey of the novel psychological observations because they are the starting point of the following excursion.

Freud turns our attention to the fact that patients who suffer from a "traumatic neurosis" (caused, for instance, by a railway disaster and other accidents) seem in their conscious thoughts not much occupied with memories of the highly unpleasant experience. (Freud adds, "Perhaps they are more concerned with not thinking of it.") Strangely enough, it is in their dreams that these patients regularly experience the frightening accident or the traumatic event. This seems to be in opposition to the wish-fulfillment function of the dream which we assumed. In other areas of human behavior we are surprised by similar phenomena: In children's play there is a very clear tendency to repeat often unpleasant experiences, mostly overpowering ones. This tendency may puzzle us, until we assume that the repetition in the play has the function of mastering the experience, of conquering it emotionally.

In the behavior of the neurotic patients we encounter the surprising fact that many of them at certain points reproduce a repressed experience instead of remembering it. It seems as if they are compelled to resurrect a piece of forgotten life—mostly in connection with the relation to the psychoanalyst—instead of, as we analysts would wish, recollecting it. They play, so to speak, the part of an actor on the stage, rather than merely reciting the text. Also, those reproduced parts of their forgotten life usually have an unpleasant character, or are overwhelming to the individual. Freud calls that astonishing aspect of behavior, observed in many patients, the "compulsion to repeat."

Of special interest to us in this context is another psychoanalytic observation that concerns not only neurotic patients but people who are normal, even as you and I. Those other instances we mentioned—the phenomena in dreams, analytic observation that concerns not only neurotic patients— are, after all, exceptional situations. But how about the everyday life of average people?

Freud has shown us that in the lives of many normal

people the mysterious repetition compulsion operates in the formation of their destiny, in the same way as in the neurotics. Freud observed many people whose relationship with others always takes the same course and shows the same outcome, although the persons they deal with are different. There are people whose relationship with their superiors, with friends, and with women go through the same phases and arrive at the same conclusion. Their partners change, but the sequence of events remain almost identical with the different persons.

It sometimes seems that a malignant fate pursues these men and women. The compulsion to repeat, which appears in their life histories, resurrects intensely unpleasurable experiences. The persons themselves apparently do not do anything to bring about their destiny. Whatever happens— and it is always the same—happens to them; it just seems to occur whatever they do or omit doing. Since these individuals show no obvious neurotic symptoms, some psychiatrists have spoken of a "neurosis of destiny" in similar cases.

We would not be too astonished to read life stories of such a strange character in novels, but here is life itself, life in the raw, not its fabricated reflection in fiction. Yet the life stories we hear are stranger than fiction.

The observation of the emergence of the compulsion to repeat, the recurrence of the same fatality—all such observations made through many years—led Freud to a definite hypothesis. There is in psychical life a tendency that operates before the pleasure principle comes into effect, before the individual strives to seek pleasure and to avoid non-pleasure. It is a strong impulse overriding that established principle of pleasure. The compulsion to repeat has the function of mastering earlier traumatic experiences of the individual, to enable him to remain in a state of emotional equilibrium.

There are still a number of questions and problems remaining. Doubtless there are other often concealed motives from the side of the ego, which sometimes cooperate with that compulsion to repeat. We recognize also that in the "neurosis of destiny" certain individual character traits often express themselves.

Here is a shaft of light that allows even a deeper insight into the nature of all drives. A new theory about them emerges. At this point all conclusions must be put aside, because we want to continue our march, or tour of exploration, into the repetition compulsion in Jewish history.

We bear in mind that an unconquered past is re-created in that compulsion. It is a certain form of remembrance of things past that are not things passé.

An Argument Is Brought Forth

May I take a giant step? May I step from these observations, made about individuals, to groups or nations? May I take this giant step? Not yet, because a powerful argument looms up. There is a decisive and essential difference between the individual life and the lives of a group, such as nations or tribes. As long as we do not dispense with this argument, our road is blocked.

This is certainly not the place to discuss the general subject of different treatment in individual and collective psychology. It will be sufficient to refer here to the works of Freud and of his students.[4] An example of that method is seen in the following paragraphs. The example is chosen at random, but we know that there is, strictly speaking, no such thing as randomness. Our choice also will be determined. We shall recognize that it is intimately connected with our subject by invisible threads.

In one of his essays Frcud discusses certain characteristic types that are met with in psychoanalytic work.[5] Persons of this type behave as if they were exceptions, exempt from the necessities of life, for whom the common rules are not valid. These patients whom Freud characterizes as "exceptions" are compared by him with Shakespeare's Richard III, who reveals his character in that famous monologue. Those strange people whom Freud so characterized base their exceptionalism on the fact that they suffered a severe traumatic experience or a serious physical handicap in earliest childhood. They feel innocent of a congenital illness or of that handicap and expect that life will compensate them for it.

After Freud has psychoanalytically interpreted the attitude of those neurotic patients with whom he compared Shakespeare's Gloucester, he adds a remark, so to speak an aside. He does not intend, he says, to discuss on this occasion "the obvious analogy with character deformation after long-lasting sickliness and with the behavior of a whole people with a past fraught with suffering." This last side glance is obviously directed to the Jewish people.

Did I not timidly ask, "May I take a giant step?" Here such a step is unhesitatingly and confidently taken. From the psychology of certain neurotic patients to the analysis of a character from Shakespeare, then to the interpretation of the emotional attitude of a whole people—what a daring leap!

No, we shall no longer shrink from comparing the compulsion to repeat, as we observe it operating in the life histories of neurotic patients, with the same power, if and when it is found, in the history of the ancient Hebrews and of the Jews. No methodological hesitancies will now prevent us from marching forward. From now on the material will speak for itself.

Where will we find the material to be explored? Where will we get hold of the convincing evidence that such a recurring fatalism, such a repetition compulsion, is also at work in the story of the Jewish people?

We must see hard facts first. Their interpretation will follow. Possibly we shall fail in our venture, but we shall not be lacking in courage. Moral courage belongs to the imperative requirements of the researcher. P. C. Bridgeman once remarked that scientists are men wrestling to do "their damnedest with their minds, no holds barred."

The Pattern

We are in trouble because we are surrounded by a vast literature on Jewish history and we should like to have a guide to tell us which book is best to choose from this immense library. Here is an abundant source of information— sometimes of misinformation—a colossal accumulation of data from the whole world of Jewry. We should now study the prehistory and the history of this people and devote years, perhaps a lifetime to it. As Arnold H. Glasgow once said:

> *Knowledge just for the knowing*
> *Is like ploughing without sowing.*

Our goal is definite. We want to find the "repetitive core" (I borrow this expression from Lawrence Kubie) of Jewish history.[6] If this is our goal, would it not be sufficient to look at the history of the Jewish people from a bird's-eye view? There are quite a few books that promise such a view, but in reading some of them you get the impression that the bird must have been a sparrow. What we need is the view of an eagle, comparable to the one on whose wings the Lord took His people out of Egypt—of an eagle who soars very high and rarely descends to grasp his prey.

Our view of Hebrew beginnings has undergone momentous changes, especially under the influence of the archaeological discoveries of the past generation. We can trace those beginnings up to the age of patriarchs. Yet even such a prominent biblical historian as William F. Albright does not dare to penetrate deeper into the prehistoric area. He points out that the traditions of Genesis, wherein the ancestors of Israel stem from Mesopotamia, have been "strikingly confirmed" by recently found linguistic data.[7]

In my view, the conjectures of biblical historians should not begin with Terah's migration from Ur to Haran, but even earlier—perhaps about the third quarter of the 20th century, B.C. According to the traditions of Genesis, the ancestors of the Hebrews were akin to the nomadic people who roamed over north Arabia in search of pasture. Arabia was the cradleland of the Semites. From there, from time immemorial, wave after wave of peoples poured forth to the more fertile contiguous lands.[8] It is very likely that we meet the ancestors of the Hebrews among the Amorites who roamed over North Africa. More about this cradleland later.

History and story pass into each other for that earliest phase from which the Hebrew people later emerge. Whether the patriarchs were real persons or only representatives of tribes is irrelevant for our view, which tries to penetrate the destiny of a people in the making. Here, only the ups and downs of those ancient Hebrew tribes are marked.

From the biblical stories in which, despite many distortions and elaborations, a historic core remains, we conclude that the sheik of some Hebrew tribe—he appears under the name of Abraham—led his people to Egypt because they were threatened by famine. Although immigrants were at first welcomed in Egypt, they were finally driven out (Genesis 12). After leaving Egypt they drifted about, but later returned to that land. Egyptian records seem to indicate that the Hyksos, a northwestern Semitic people who were akin to the Hebrews and who had conquered Egypt before 1750 B.C., favored the Hebrew tribes. It is not unlikely that some of them reached high positions, like Joseph, according to the tradition.

Then came the turn. The Hyksos were crushed by Amosis I. Amosis is perhaps the "Pharaoh who knew not Joseph" (Exodus 1:8).

It is likely that some Hebrew leaders and their followers escaped to Palestine; the people who remained were reduced to bondage, forced into labor in the region of the long-neglected city of Tanis (in the land of Goshen).

Many thousands of Hebrew slaves worked in and around that new Egyptian capital. The impressive figure of Moses appears at this time, and the picture is changed. He led the army of serfs and slaves and many others of similar origin through the wilderness of the Sinai Peninsula. These people who escaped the Egyptian oppression and survived many dangers formed the tribal nucleus of the new people of Israel.

Those few sentences perhaps describe the succession of events of many hundreds of years of history, or rather pre-history, of the Hebrew tribes. They already give the impression of a miniature picture in anticipation of the spectacle of future millennia. Here we see the immigration into a foreign country, the attainment to high position, the turning to hostility on the part of the host nation, then bondage and expulsion. The story ends with the flight from Egypt under the leadership of Moses, but behind that glorious story is the image of Egyptian persecution, of a long period of wandering, of battles, and of entering a new land.

In this initial phase of Jewish history, in this half-mythical prehistory, the essential characteristic features of the future are already evident. We recognize the traits that will be fateful for the millennia to come. This initial phase has the earmarks of a past that will refuse to become a memory.

We follow the next two thousand years in a highly telescopic manner: the period of judges and kings, the quarrels among the tribes, the Philistine raids, and the splitting of the country into two neighboring states of Judah and Israel.

Should we stop at this point? A German writer, Frank Wedekind, once remarked that the ability to form and to maintain a state is not within the capabilities of the Jewish people. (A facetious saying has it that when two Jews enter into a discussion they have three different opinions.)

This defect—if defect it is—was also characteristic of the ancient Hebrews. The two states had a short duration of life. They were threatened by aggressive neighbors, but even more by the rivalries and jealousies among the tribes themselves. It was not difficult for the Assyrians to conquer

Israel and to deport her people. The kingdom of Judah, an area the size of New Hampshire, was also soon captured. The Babylonians, newly replacing the Assyrians in power, took the Jews into exile. They remained in Babylon for more than a century, and only a part of them returned to Palestine, then under the Persian empire. A great number remained in Babylon. In Persia quite a few Jews achieved high places at the king's court (consider the story of Esther) but they soon suffered persecution.

We rapidly pass over the Greek period, the capture of the country by the Romans, and the final conquest in 70 B.C.

During the times of the Greek and Roman empires there were a significant number of favored Jews who distinguished themselves, but the end was always the same.

There are recurring cycles, ups and downs, but the course of events is essentially the same, with small variations. It has been said that history repeats itself. This is perhaps not quite correct; it merely rhymes.

Besides, the content and the form of aggressiveness in the host nations changed to some extent, but essentially it was the same, as Haman expressed it when speaking to King Ahasuerus (Esther 3:8): "There is a certain people scattered abroad and dispersed among the people in all the provinces of thy kingdom; and their laws are diverse from all people; neither keep they the king's laws. . . ."

The era of the diaspora of the Jewish people, of their dispersion throughout the world, began many centuries before Titus burned the Temple of Jerusalem in the year 70 B.C. But their exile in the real sense began then. The Jews were dispersed among other countries of Asia, Africa, and Europe. They were outside the country which had been their home for some millennia.

So a new chapter begins, dealing with the destinies of the Jewish groups in various countries, separated from each other by thousands of miles. Will those Jews follow the same pattern everywhere?

Early Anti-Judaism

Before we go on, let us take a rapid side glance at anti-Semitic tendencies in early antiquity.

As a matter of fact, there was little anti-Judaism in the writings of the ancient world. Wherever Jews are mentioned, they were treated neutrally and sometimes even benevolently. A student of Aristotle, reported that his teacher had made the acquaintance of a Jew who not only in language but also in his mind, was a Greek and from whom he had derived much wisdom.[9] What Aristotle meant is clear: that Jew was not a barbarian at all; on the contrary, he was a wise man.

Yet in the second century before Christ expressions of anti-Judaism are evident in the writings of Greek and later of Roman authors. Pliny calls . . . them a people who abuse the divinity. Tacitus asserts that they are averse to religion.[10] He reproaches them for not sharing table and bed with the women of other people.[11]

The picture of the Jew as the ancient world saw it and as we encounter it in Posidonius, Cicero, and the Roman poets is mostly satirical. There is the mockery about their laziness on the Sabbath and their aversion to pork. Yet the attitude toward the Jews is ambivalent even with Tacitus,

who admires them because there are no images of God in
their cities and sanctuaries.[12]

How is such an attitude of some Greek and, to a greater
extent, Roman writers since the second century to be explained? In his book *Genèse de l'Antisemitism* Jules Isaac
points out that the victorious march of Hellenistic civilization encountered the unexpected resistance of the Macca-
bees when King Antiochus IV (175-164) tried to reform
the Jews.[13] Tacitus is of the opinion that Antiochus wished
to do away with their superstitions and make them familiar
with Greek mores in order to improve a most stubborn
people. Posidonius reports that the councilors of Antiochus
VII declared that the Jews, of all people, were the only ones
who rejected all social relationships with other people. Isaac
thinks that the main accusation of the pagan anti-Semitism
emerges as the natural and inevitable consequence of the
strict isolation which the Torah, and especially in the diaspora, dictates to Israel.

Concerning the attitude of the Persians and of the man
Haman toward the Jews, we have already remarked on the
Book of Esther (3:8).

Late antiquity thus shows a decided ambivalence toward
the Jews. They were privileged by Alexander and by most of
the Ptolemies, by Caesar and Augustus and their successors.
Caligula, Claudius, Nero, Trajan, and Hadrian tried to
"civilize" them. All in all, the pre-Christian era considered
the Jews a self-sufficient minority, admired and hated, and
at the same time often tolerated and sometimes even
privileged by the authorities.

As a wanderer bound for a certain destination stops a
few minutes to look at interesting scenery, we were led
astray by the view of early manifestations of anti-Judaism
in antiquity. Let us now continue our march back into the
past of Jewry.

In the Dispersion

Every avenue was open to the refugees. Many remained in Mesopotamia under Persian rule. In the first centuries of the Christian era, there were perhaps millions of Jews living in Babylonia, where they were almost autonomous. While their situation was very good at first, their condition worsened and they were persecuted during the sixth century. In France, where many Jews settled since Roman times, local bishops enforced mass baptism. In Greece, southern Italy, and North Africa, Emperor Heraclius (610-641) tried to convert them to Catholicism. King Dagobert did the same in Gaul.

Under the regime of the Visigoths, the Jews in Spain, where many had settled, were at first favored, but were later forced to convert. Those who remained faithful to their religion were driven out.

The Islamitic countries were friendly to the Jews. The Mohammedans treated them cordially and Jewish poets enriched the Arabic literature. Later on, in the time of the Caliphs, Jews and Christians were subjected to heavy taxes and other restrictions. Also in Spain, where Jews had followed the Arabian conquerors as colonists, traders, and so on, they were initially favored and had important positions as physicians, counselors, poets, and statesmen. All this changed after 1055 when the Christians captured Toledo. Fanatic Mohammedans forced the conversion of many Jews to Islam. The same happened also in North Africa from which many Jews fled.

The Emperor Charles the Great encouraged the immigration of Jewish merchants and showed preference for them. Among the Carolingians many were sent out as interpreters and were protected by the kings. The south of France be came one of the centers of Jewish life. Also Cologne, Augsburg, and Prague saw them prospering at the close of the eleventh century. Many Jews had gone to England where they lived in London, Oxford, and Bristol. Everywhere the importance of Jewish contributions to culture increased. The revival of Arabic literature owes much to the Jews, among whom such great poets as ibn-Gabirol, Abraham ben Meir ibn Ezra, Judah ha-Levi, scholars such as Rashi in Troy and Moses Maimonides were acknowledged.

The crusades changed all that. The Christian zeal to win Palestine back for the Cross marked a phase of martyrdom for the Jews. In the cities on the Rhine, in Speyer, Worms, and elsewhere entire Jewish communities were exterminated. The Jews in Jerusalem were driven into a synagogue and burned to death. From the Rhine to France massacres of the Jews took place. The persecutions even reached England where Jewish refugees had previously been welcomed. Many English cities witnessed the death of thousands of Jews. In Italy Jews had a comparatively good life— they were numerous, especially in Sicily—until the House of Anjou took the kingdom of Naples and began to persecute them.

In Spain, where the Jews were prominent as scientists, physicians and financiers, their prosperity reached its zenith under Alfonso of Castile (1109). The Jews were generally on an equal basis with gentiles. Here again the crusades of the thirteenth century marked the turning point. Victorious Christianity led to attacks against the Jews, and the more the Moslems were pushed back, the more the Jews were subjected to restrictions.

Before 1200, expulsion of the Jews was actually unknown. In England in 1201 they enjoyed liberty. Yet once again the libel of ritual murder led to massacres and bloody riots. The restrictions of the Fourth Lateran Council were enforced with the greatest severity in France, where, around 1300, all Jews were condemned to exile.

The crusades, as well as the accusation that the Jews desecrated the Host and murdered children during Passover, led to terrible attacks against them in Germany and Austria. The Black Death, around the year 1348, was laid at the door of the Jews. In the series of massacres that followed, many German and Austrian Jewish communities were exterminated, such as during the attack in the Judengasse in Vienna where previously the Jews had enjoyed privileges.

In Spain and Portugal, where Jews had been favored for a long time, 70,000 Jews were killed, many thousands forcibly converted. The Marranos (Christianized Jews) gained great influence and rose to important positions at the universities, at the court, and even within the Church.

Yet many of them were punished in auto-da-fés where they were burned to death. (The first auto-da-fé was in Seville in 1481.) The auto-da-fés formed the prologue to the tribunal of the Holy Inquisition in Spain. Torquemada was the first inquisitor general. Three thousand neo-Christians were denounced on account of Judaizing. All Jews were expelled from the dominions in 1492. About 150,000 people left Spain and fled to other countries. Many found a place of refuge in Italy and contributed abundantly to the flowering of the Renaissance. Jewish scientists and scholars (for instance, León Hebreo who died in 1535), physicians and philosophers became famous. Hebrew books could be printed.

Martin Luther had at first favored the Jews, but then turned against them. He wanted the synagogues to be burned down and declared the Talmud a blasphemous book.

When Cardinal Carafa became Pope Paul IV, he issued a bull (in 1555) in which he segregated the Jews in ghettoes and excluded them from certain professions. The Counter Reformation put great pressure on the Jews as well.

Eastern Jewry was shaken by the Cossack massacres of the Jews in the Ukraine. When the Czar of Russia invaded Poland in 1634, the Jewish residents of White Russia and Lithuania were exterminated or expelled. The refugees fled in terror to the West, where their position seemed to be much better.

With the Enlightenment, the ghetto was removed. Joseph II of Germany published the Edict of Toleration in 1781, whereby the Jews became almost equal to other citizens.

The anti-Jewish campaign started in Germany again when Bismarck became Chancellor and the court and cathedral preacher Adolf Stoecker denounced the Jewish domination, emphasizing the superiority of the Teutonic race. Episodes such as the Eslar ritual murder prosecutions and the Dreyfus case were less terrifying to the Jews than the regulations enforced by the Russian government of Alexander II. Expulsion from certain districts, prohibition against Jewish women in the large cities except as declared prostitutes were only a part of these. After 1890 pogroms against the Jews were the order of the day. Many thousands of Jews were murdered. A new exodus began. The refugees turned to England and America, where many of them or their descendants reached prominent positions.

In the European War of 1914 numerous Jewish communities were destroyed. The czarist General Denikin promulgated bloody pogroms in which a quarter of a million Jews fell victim. The Bolshevik Revolution in 1917 was no milder in its attitude toward the Jews.

Yet none of this is comparable to the holocaust the Nazis brought about. The total destruction of Eastern Jewry and the murder of seven million Jews was only part of the unprecedented cruelties committed by Hitler and his minions.

These are the dry and indisputable facts, purposely presented in this tightly compressed form. In sober and naked character they make up the dossier we now examine.

The Recurring Pattern

Despite the differences and diversities of time and place, of variations conditioned by geographical, sociological and psychological factors, a very definite pattern in the course of Jewish history can be seen. This recurring pattern becomes plain in earliest antiquity during the prehistoric phase of the Hebrew tribes, and reaches into our own time, into the days of the Nazi regime whose horrified witnesses we have been. I do not doubt that the same pattern will govern the lives of our grandchildren, unless unexpected and revolutionary changes take place.

As the French say, *"Plus ça change, plus c'est la même chose"* (the more things change, the more they remain the same). We acknowledge, of course, the great differences brought about by time and progress, but we believe that the "repetitive core" (to use Lawrence Kubie's felicitous expression once more) of the sequence of events in Jewish history is recognizable throughout the millennia.

What is that repetitive core? In simplest terms it is the following: The Jews immigrate into a new country (Egypt,

Palestine, Greece, Germany), sometimes as welcome guests, where in a short time they become prominent in science, medicine, literature, commerce and finance. Some acquire high social position. The envy of the host people is then awakened and increases to hostility. A secret storm starts brewing. Often an insignificant incident has a triggering effect and unleashes the storm. There are accusations against the foreigners, and finally outbreaks of violence, riots, pogroms and massacres. The end is always the same. The Jews are either exterminated or are forced to leave the country.

We have seen the fate of the Jews in many lands. Their story has a definite beginning, a middle, and an end like a classic tragedy. Even prehistory reveals the fatal pattern. Abraham came to Egypt, gained the patronage of the Pharaoh, and was then asked to leave the country. Isaac sowed in the land and prospered; "he grew until he became very great." The Philistines envied him (Genesis 26:14), Abimelech, King of the Philistines, "said unto Isaac 'Go from us; for thou art much mightier than we.'" Again the expulsion. Moses, educated at the Egyptian court, possibly became governor of a province. Eventually he and his people had to flee Egypt, pursued by the army. Joseph gained high position at the court and brought his whole family to Egypt. When other pharaohs came to power, however, Joseph's people had to leave.

As we go from this phase of prehistory to the most recent period, we see the same picture. In Germany and Austria, Jews distinguished themselves in many professions and areas of research (Freud, Einstein, and many more) and enriched German civilization. The bitter end was annihilation in the gas chambers; for the more fortunate, escape to safety in other countries.

The impression we get is that of a *Schicksalsneurose* (neurosis of destiny) of a whole group or nation, a fateful succession analogous to what we observe in the life stories of certain individuals. The next question is, of course: Is that repetitive core significant and meaningful?

Although I have not found any book or paper that discusses or even takes note of the repetition compulsion in Jewish history, there are many books, even whole libraries, on the peculiarity of the Jewish fate, written by Jews and Christians. All seek a meaning in that peculiar and special course evident in Jewish history. Is there such a meaning at all, or is that strange fate merely the result of blind mechanical forces at work in world history?

What is the oldest interpretation of that peculiarity in Jewish history? It is to be found in the Holy Scriptures. There can be no doubt that its authors were Jews who saw their present or future destiny as directed by God, determined by divine control. It does not surprise us that most of those declarations are pronounced by the Voice of Voices itself, while others are proclaimed by His chosen prophets. Their character is one of delivering messages fraught with visions of terrible disaster, in which all the evils befalling the Jews are conceived as just punishment for their sins, especially for their disobedience to God and for their inflexible obstinacy—"Because I knew that thou art obstinate, and thy neck is an iron sinew" (Isaiah 48:4).

Following are a few of those Biblical verses chosen at random: "And the Lord shall scatter thee among all people, from the one end of the earth even unto the other; . . . And among those nations shalt thou have no repose, and there be no rest for the sole of thy foot; but the Lord shall give thee there a trembling heart, and failing of eyes, and sorrow of mind; And thy life shall hang in doubt before thee; and thou shalt fear day and night, and shalt have no assurance of thy life" (Deuteronomy 28:64-66). Moses already foresees that the Jews "shalt become an astonishment, a proverb, and a byword, among all nations whither the Lord shall lead thee" (Deuteronomy 28:37)—a prophecy that was literally fulfilled.

It is well known how the Christians conceived the fate of the Jews: Because the Jews rejected Christ, they were punished. These people must be preserved until the end of time as witnesses of the Cross. It is said that the freethinking Frederick the Great, who admired Voltaire, once asked Count C. F. Reventlow in sarcasm: "Can you name me a single incontrovertible proof of God?" "Yes, Majesty," answered the count; "the Jews."

Millions of people still accept this proof. There is no question here for Christian and Jewish theologians nor for the believers of both faiths. Jewish history is the prelude to the salvation connected with the coming of Christ, in the view of the gentiles. For believing Jews, their history is the promise of the coming of the Messiah.

To pursue a practice we have previously adopted, sayings of ancient times are contrasted with expressions of recent writers. In Nicolai Berdyaev's *Christianity and Anti-Semitism,* which appeared in 1952, this eminent Russian thinker points out how paradoxical Jewish destiny is.[14] They have no earthly kingdom or state, "a privilege enjoyed by the most insignificant of people"; they feel chosen, and suffer only contempt and persecution. Their whole destiny presents a perpetual crucifixion. While they reject the Cross, they must carry it, "while those who welcomed it are often engaged in burdening them with it. . . . The Jews rejected Christ, but were the first to follow him; the Apostles were Jews. . . ."[15]

Berdyaev reproaches Christians for their unwillingness to acknowledge the Jews as a people with a unique religious destiny. The doctrine of the chosen people is "a privilege of responsibility." It implies that the Jewish people assume "the yoke of the kingdom of God."

We are painfully aware of having left out of our discussion the views of many Jewish philosophers and mystics, even of some important writers such as Martin Buber, as well as of Christian theologians. Moreover, the opinions of sociologists, psychologists and anthropologists have not been taken into account. This would have presented a task that would have protracted our march—not merely delaying it with frequent halts, dwelling on significant points along the way, but would have burdened us with a tremendous load.

Rather than quote the views of ancient, medieval, and modern theologians, we limit ourselves to a glimpse at a most recent trial, to the criminal case of Adolf Eichmann. The following very short interlude will show that theologians and philosophers were not the only ones who tried to pass the buck to God and to some divine mysterious power.

Interlude

In his opening address, Gideon Hauser began his presentation with the persecution of the Hebrews by Pharaoh and Haman's decree "to destroy, to slay, and to cause them to perish." He quoted Ezekiel, "And when I passed by thee and saw thee polluted in thine blood, I said unto thee 'In thy blood, live,' " and explained that these words must be understood as "the imperative that has confronted this nation ever since its first appearance on the stage of history." [16]

A few sessions later Salo Baron, professor of Jewish his-

tory at Columbia University, testified to the recent history of
Eastern European Jewry. After this survey, Dr. Robert Servatius for the defense asked the witness, "Can you, Professor,
give reasons for this negative treatment of the Jewish people?" Baron then discussed the major theories on the origin
of anti-Semitism, pointed to Judaism as a minority religion,
mentioned economic reasons and jealousy of prominent people. He himself considered the "dislike of the unlike" as the
main reason of anti-Judaism. The Jews became the national
scapegoat when anything went wrong with individuals and
nations.

Then Dr. Servatius in all innocence asked the second
question: "Don't you think, Professor, that underlying the
fate of the Jewish people are irrational forces, beyond human understanding?"

We shall not present the ensuing erudite discussion between Baron and Servatius, with quotations from Hegel,
Spencer, Savigny, and Marx; let us stop at this point. The
intention of the defense counsel was obvious. If the persecution of the Jews has been preordained, if their fate was directed by remote divine control, then Eichmann was only a
pawn on God's chessboard. Yes, he would perhaps even deserve a medal, especially since (here is Dr. Servatius' last
question) the intent to destroy was foiled and a flourishing
state came into being instead.

The whole discussion interests us here only in so far as
we recognize in Dr. Servatius' question a very modernized
variation of an old view concerning fatalism in Jewish history. We do not believe in that divine remote control, and
can thus without the least scruple of conscience dismiss this
aspect of the Jewish problem.

Ahasuerus

Let us dwell briefly on one of the final results of the "repetitive core," namely, on the recurring migrations of the Jews. That curse in Deuteronomy was very impressive; it foresaw the dispersion and predicted the Jewish wanderings. What is the meaning of the Diaspora, and what is the significance of those recurring migrations?

The original migration of the Hebrews was not enforced by their enemies as were those of recent times. Famine drove them from Arabia to Mesopotamia, and it was famine again that brought Abraham to Egypt.

George Eliot, whose insights sometimes astonished Freud, has one of her Jewish characters in *Daniel Deronda* say, "Our people wandered before they were driven out." What secret is connected with those wanderings that have continued until our day? The Jews wandered thus three thousand years and are still going—or rather wandering—strong.

As early as the first century, Roman historians reported how the Jews had penetrated all countries and how difficult it was to find a single place where they had not been. But the Galuth or the Exile is much older than this. We find a Jewish Aramaic-speaking colony in Egypt, in Elephantine, after the nation's collapse. At least one million Jews were in Egypt after they had followed Alexander the Great on his expeditions and after they had settled in Alexandria. A hundred thousand of them were fully assimilated to Greek culture. After the return of the Jews from Babylonia with Egra, Babylonia remained a second Jewish cultural center besides Jerusalem.

The Diaspora through France, Germany, Spain, and other countries has already been sketched. Spanish travelers encountered children in the Levant who had never seen Spain, yet spoke pure Castilian. North Africa absorbed many thousands of Jews after the expulsion from Spain, as did Turkey, and then America at a later date.

Jews settled in Poland in the thirteenth century and Casimir the Great used them for the reconstruction of the country to such an extent that he was called "King of the serfs and the Jews." A Jewish legion later fought for Poland and was almost wiped out.

This brings us to the threshold of our own time, and so to the massacres by the Hitler army and the most recent exodus.

The prophetic conception of the dispersion, as expressed in the Old Testament, is continued and modified in the Ahasuerus legend. According to the tale, a Jewish shoemaker chased Christ who was carrying his cross, from the threshold of his house and was cursed by the Savior to wander forever without dying. This legend of the Eternal Jew, traced to its sources by Moncure Daniel Conway, has many variations, and was later often used for anti-Jewish purposes.[17]

Free association leads me at this point to a recently published historical novel, *The Emperor, the Sages, and Death*, by Rachel Berdach, in which an interesting variation of the old Ahasuerus motif appears.[18] There a Jewish tale is told of the young Rabbi Jehoshua, stumbling under his cross to the place of execution. He stopped at the house of an old man, called the Sage. The Rabbi turned to this man and to his little grandson and said that he must not rest now. "You must not rest either," he continued, "nor must this child. No Jew should rest, but you shall wander until the Messiah comes to the world. Say't to your friends, carry it to the people, that they shall wander, that they shall teach, when all men are united, shall Israel find its peace." The Rabbi placed his hand on the boy's head and blessed him.

But all such interpretations are obviously of a religious nature, whereas we are searching for a rational and scientific explanation of the Jewish migrations. It is evident that such an explanation has to be based on the whole past, because we know that the migrations of our times—for instance the new exodus following the Nazi terror—were dictated by the persecution of the Jewish people. But we find the Jews wandering before they were oppressed and restricted. Religious intolerance, envy, and hostility of the host nations, although certainly of decisive importance, do not fully explain that intensive tendency to go from one country to another. We must find other determining factors besides those mentioned. We have perhaps neglected the psychological agents at work in the history of the Jewish people.

There is an old song hit of Maurice Chevalier, *"On est comme on est."* Yes, we are as we are, but also we are as we became.

The only study, as far as I know, that presents such a psychological theory, based on the past, is by Kadmi Cohen, who calls his book *Nomade*s and gives it the subtitle *"Essai sur l'âme Juive."* [19] The author points out that nomadic people are the only ones who do not depend on the soil. Man, he says, is "the male of the earth, the earth his mistress and his nutritive maintainer." Soon he will become her slave, will become dependent on her, the earth, which is his most important property. (In contrast to the nomad whose only possession is the portable tent.) The battle between the two tendencies of settling on the soil and freedom to leave is reflected in the biblical story of Cain and Abel.

The Jew of the twentieth century has that tendency to migration, *"ce goût des migrations"* as well as his ancestor three thousand years ago. A passage in the Old Testament is considered very significant by Kadmi Cohen. The Lord proclaims: "The land is mine; for ye are strangers and sojourners with me" (Leviticus 25:23).

The French writer discovers other characteristic traits of the Semitic nomads. There is, for instance, the spirit of personal insubordination. Neither the Arabic nor the Hebrew language has a word to express the idea of discipline. (The modern Hebrew knows the word *mischuca,* which is derived from "to hear.") When the ancient Hebrews wanted a king rather than judges, the Lord said unto Samuel: "Hearken unto the voice of the people in all that they say unto thee; for they have not rejected thee, but they have rejected me, that I should not reign over them. According to all the works which they have done since the day that I brought them up out of Egypt, even unto this day wherewith they have forsaken me, and served other gods, so do they also unto thee" (I Samuel 8:7-8). This is psychologically very significant.

Even the authority of the Lord is not acknowledged. There is an open rebellion against Him, too. While the other civilizations are based on the establishment of a principle of external authority which is itself sovereign (*"sur un principe d'autorité exterieure, souverain en soi"*), the Semitic nomads had nothing comparable. This stiff-necked people do not know any inherited nobility, no private possession, nor landed property. For the ancient Jews the myth of Antaeus would make no sense. Kadmi Cohen finds signs of that intense aversion to private property also in the teachings of Marx, Lasalle, Leon Blum, and others.

There are other characteristic features of the Semitic nomads. The Hebrew has no proper word for suicide. The Talmud knows only one reason for suicide, namely, insanity. Life is the supreme aim. Renan spoke of an *"intoler-ance sémitique"* and of a *"culte de l'homme."* George A. Bar-ton says of the Semites, "Nothing seems to them so divine as the power to give life. . . . They deifed that power." [20] This tendency "is seen in that delight in offspring and devotion to family that is characteristic of Jews to this day." [21] "It is this which makes every Arab jubilant at the birth of a son." The care for the perpetuation of race has been among Sem-ites "all-pervasive and persistent."

(By the way, George A. Barton would also agree with the previously quoted statement of Frank Wedekind, that the Jews lacked political genius. Barton says, "It has been well said that the "Semitic form of government was a despotism tempered by assassination. . . . There are inherent weak-nesses in such a political order. Every Semitic state has led a checkered career, and the Semites have contributed little to the political philosophy of the world. . . . The aptitude for such leadership was apparently not theirs.")

The task of the Semites and especially of the Jews was of a different kind.

Kadmi Cohen asserts that the Bedouin patriarchs made way for the greatest religions of the world. Among all the tribes of the Semitic nomads, the Hebrews were already marked for a tremendous destiny. (*"Entre toutes les tribus de Semites nomades, celle de Beni Israel était déjà marquée pour d'immenses destinées."*)

The Renunciation

So the arguments of this writer are, if not convincing, persuasive. He has certainly caught certain characteristic traits of the Semitic nomads, but when we consider the realities as history presents them, we become skeptical. The descendants of those Arabic nomads are just now establishing a United Arabic Republic under Nasser, whom they consider authority not to be disputed. There is not much equality and social justice to be observed in these people. The old feudal system is still in force everywhere.

As an explanation of the dispersion of the Jews throughout the world, the logic of the French writer is certainly inadequate. None of those nomadic Semitic tribes were dispersed to all the continents and in all the countries of the Old and New World. The Arabs wandered, but within narrow confines—no exile and no diaspora.

There must be other factors operating to explain the dispersion of the Jews.

Before we discuss them, we should like to make a few remarks about certain aspects neglected in the sagacious considerations of Kadmi Cohen. It seems to me that he has not pointed out—or else not emphasized enough—that the ancient Hebrews, at least those of later time, renounced power of a secular character. They denied themselves the glory and the enjoyment of political might.

Everyone who aspires to one thing must renounce others. This explains the character of ambition, especially its singleness of purpose and its exclusion of other aims. In the case of the Jews, the pursuit of social justice became their ultimate aim in the time of the prophets. "Not by might, nor by power, but by my spirit, saith the Lord of hosts" (Zechariah 4:6). Zechariah, who proclaims this message, lived during the time of the Persian King Darius.

Having confessed to a penchant for contrasting the most ancient with the new, I would like to refer to a play by the modern poet Richard Beer-Hofmann, *Jacobs Traum*.[22] In the second act of the play in which Jacob faces the Lord, he speaks for himself as well as for his people:

> *Finds He no use for us but to be kings?*
> *I will not rule. Does He not know?*
> *Mizraem, Babel and the sea-lands prince*
> *Can He believe I envy them their goods?*

In the grandiose vision of the patriarch resounds the same renunciation of wordly power that the prophets proclaimed. The new Arab Republic under Nasser suggests nothing of such a renunciation. On the contrary: these descendants of nomads do not conceal their lust for conquest, their urge for expansion.

Have we now cleared the way for an interpretation of the Jewish diaspora? The view of Kadmi Cohen is impressive but does not trace certain traits of character of the Jewish people back far enough to its historic or rather prehistoric time. When he referred to the nomadic character of the Jewish people he sounded a chord, but did he play it to the end of the melody?

At this point a recollection intrudes. My brother Otto, fifteen years older than I, sometimes brought a friend home from school. I was a little boy at the time and knew the young man only as Arnold. His name was Arnold Schönberg who afterward became a great composer, perhaps the most important after Gustave Mahler. Much later I was told that Schönberg, listening to his students' compositions sometimes remarked, *"Das ist nicht ausgehört,"* which meant that it was not heard with complete insight to the end. His young students either did not take the time or were too impatient to follow the melody they had conceived to its end, to listen to its continuation and development with the inner ear.

Kadmi Cohen—to continue the figure of speech—heard a certain melody, but he did not hear it to its organic end. It was not *"ausgehört."* Otherwise he would have recognized that this psychological theory about nomadic characteristics does not explain the dispersal of the Jewish people. It is only when we add that the Jews renounced political power that we are able to realize where they were going, what their real aim was. Also, for the Jews, the world was once their oyster, but oysters are forbidden food according to their dietary laws.

Now the way to a psychoanalytic interpretation of the phenomenon is open, and we return to the hypothesis of a dark compulsion toward repetition which Freud found in the life history of many persons. In the individual it was the expression and re-enactment of an unconquered traumatic event, of an inescapable past. What is the analogy in the fate of groups?

The Repercussions

The Past That Refused to Become Memory

Oliver St. John Gogarty tells the story of a man who travels East to get a grandfather clock.[23] The train arrives late and the man hastens to the antique dealer from whom he buys a grandfather clock that is easily seven feet tall. "I am staying only half a block away," says the man; "send it around at once." The dealer regretfully cannot deliver it because it is late. The best thing he can offer is to send it the following day. But the purchaser does not wish to be separated from the clock. The dealer, looking the husky man over, suggests that the clock, which looks heavy but is hollow, be strapped to the man's back and it can thus be transported half a block.

The suggestion is accepted and the grandfather clock is strapped on. Not far from the shop a drunken man is thrown out of a house and collides with the clock, which is smashed to bits in the middle of the street. The man with the wrecked clock indignantly asks the drunkard, "Why don't you look where you're going?" The drunkard answers, "Why don't you wear a wristwatch like everybody else?"

The Jew is like the man wearing a grandfather clock on his back. Why must he walk around carrying a grandfather clock instead of wearing a wristwatch like everybody else?

The answer is easily given: because he is governed by the compulsion to repeat. The pattern of his life remains the same. He is compelled to re-enact events he does not remember. He must do this because in this way alone can he achieve a belated emotional mastery of certain events that disturbed his early life. Re-enacting old defeats, regardless of current problems, is emotionally imperative. He has to re-live certain traumatic events. What were the experiences that agitated these people so violently? We can only guess at them and reconstruct them from the nature of the repetitions to which their descendants were subjected. At least we can form a serious and articulate conjecture, based on the little we know.

The tribes from which the Hebrews originated at one time had an area for themselves, from which they migrated. We remember again what that character in George Eliot's novel said—"Our people wandered before they were driven out."

The nomads were not always nomads, not always people that moved from place to place in search of pasture for their cattle. The barrenness of the land that had become desert forced them to leave and wander to Mesopotamia and later to Egypt. We know that the Semitic tribes, the ancestors of the Hebrews, had their home in Arabia, from which they moved because of periods of aridity. The interior of the Arabian desert, once so fertile, became arid as the result of sand storms in prehistoric times. (Elsworth Huntington showed us that waves of emigrants went from there over the border of Palestine.)[24]

The best analogy to this conjecture is seen in the Negev, the desert area in the south of Israel. Paleobotanists at the University of Jerusalem recently discovered hundreds of fossil plants in this part of the country. Dr. Jacob Lorch and students of the Hebrew University have recovered numerous specimens of fossil plants. The conclusion toward which paleobotanists are more and more inclined is that the Negev was at one time rich in vegetation, that it was in fact a kind of garden. The fossil plants tell a fascinating story. Something like it may have happened to the original Arabian home of the Semitic tribes from which the Hebrews emerged.

Professor A. Reifenberg of the Hebrew University discussed the age-old conflict between famine and civilization, and he points to the hot, dry winds (khamsin) as being especially detrimental to vegetation.[25] The fate of the land determines the fate of the people living in it.

Let us dwell upon some of these points. This must also have happened to other tribes that, unlike the Jews, did not afterward develop a compulsion for eternal wandering. Let me clarify the nature of this difference by comparing it with the life of an individual—that is to say, with the various impressions certain decisive events make in the life of a child. It certainly makes a difference whether parents are divorced when their child is three years old or thirteen. Other than this, it matters a great deal if a child is suddenly weaned from mother's breast because she can no longer give milk. We know from clinical observations that children who are thus suddenly weaned develop differently from those who make the transition naturally from breast feeding to other food.

The decay and aridity of the original home of those Semitic tribes was in its consequences comparable to such an abrupt weaning process. It is more than a *façon de parler* when we speak of "mother earth" and of the "good earth."

There is still another factor: The conglomeration of tribes from which the Hebrews later descended—mainly Amorites —apparently belonged to the last wave of Semitic migrations leaving Arabia. Most other Semitic peoples had left the same area many hundreds, perhaps thousands, of years before. Here also the comparison with individual life is easily made. It certainly makes a difference if a boy grows up as the firstborn or as the fourth in the order of brothers.

Clinical experience shows us that the order of birth in a family of siblings is of considerable importance. When the Hebrews came to Mesopotamia and Egypt, they saw civilizations that were a few thousand years older than their own primitive organization. The feeling with which a Hebrew nomad looked at the miracle-building in Thebes, for instance, is comparable to that of a Jew who comes directly from a Russian ghetto and sees a skyscraper for the first time. He will have similar feelings when he makes the acquaintance of the many technological devices previously unknown to him.

I am sure that the ideas presented here are controversial. It is possible that they will be killed by silence. But perhaps they will be discussed, and certainly more often "cussed," by historians, theologians, archaeologists, and others. The fact that it has been maintained for over forty years is no proof of the correctness of a hypothesis, but it may be remarkable that a person's convictions should waver in that length of time without being shaken.

Further repercussions of that first traumatic experience of the Hebrew tribes will be considered later. This is perhaps the appropriate place to add one more note to a comparison attempted previously. I said that the Hebrew tribes possibly formed the last migratory wave from Arabia to the Euphrates-Nile valley. They were, so to speak, the youngest brothers of many who had followed this route many hundred years before them.

The train of thought accompanying this comparison went even further back than the previous ones. It led me back to a certain fairy-tale motif found in the stories of Grimm, Andersen, and, if memory does not fail me, also in the Arabian Nights.

This typical fairy-tale motif which exists in many variations simply says that the youngest of three or more brothers leaves them behind and proves himself superior to them by his intelligence, shrewdness, or other qualities. The psychological premise for this typical motif is obvious: The youngest brother is envious of and competitive with the older ones and strives to reach and even to surpass them. He is often more ambitious than they. He is sometimes favored by his father, and his position in the sequence of brothers frequently arouses his incentive to accomplish more. Perhaps the comparison of the Jews and other peoples with brothers will become significant. Possibly we will have another occasion to discuss the subject.

A Strange Regression

There is more than one side to a story—to the story of the Hebrews as well. We shall turn our attention to those other, neglected sides later on. This is the place for a few personal remarks.

Having written the foregoing paragraphs, I was suddenly reminded that I had conceived and written a very similar theory many decades ago. In a book *Der eigene und der fremde Gott,*[26] written in 1922, published in Vienna in 1923, not yet translated into English, I had already advanced the theory of the traumatic experience discussed in the preceding chapter. In this book, treating the relationship of people with their own God and with the God of others, a new hypothesis had been introduced: that certain unconsciously maintained and ever renewed series of experiences that must be traced back to the childhood phase of these tribes are subject to such repetitions. Freud must have spoken of repetition compulsion long before he wrote *Beyond the Pleasure Principle*. I remember a private conversation in 1921 in which he said that the United States repeats in its history the conflict with the South and the problem of intervention in Europe. He conceives that these two contentions are repetitions of earlier American experiences. Even now the antagonism to the South manifests itself in the question of segregation. The problem of intervention in Europe was still hotly debated during World War II.

I translate from the German: "I anticipate here the result of other papers: the earliest denial recognizable to us is to be seen in relation to the country, to the soil. The famine into which the sparse products of the soil forced them, I would put side by side with later important factors as the determining tendency of the primal repression that operated together with secondary agents. . . ." [27]

Here we have an early reference to the compulsion to repeat and the comparison with the analytic observation of the individual. Also, the theory is advanced that an entire people may follow that dark repetition compulsion. Certain inferences were also made, for instance, "When we consider that important reverberating experience of earliest time and the repetition compulsion striving to conquer it emotionally, we understand that the Jews later again and again lost their home and were compelled to migrate, which means, to try to regain the lost primal home."

This was written more than forty years ago and I had entirely forgotten it. I was reminded of it by my son, who read this manuscript.

This is a good confirmation of a statement I heard Freud once make, namely, that we easily forget what we have written because it is intellectually conquered and dismissed. I was astonished that those early experiences had not been explored by historians. Yet it is really not surprising. Daniel Webster once remarked, "There is nothing so powerful as truth—and often nothing so strange."

Another Prehistoric Traumatic Experience

Field Marshal Hermann Göring once expressed the wish to go to Poland to do some hunting. The British ambassador, most innocently, asked, "Animals, I presume?" At that time it was already doubtful whether animals or men were being hunted and killed. Only a short time before, the German Jews were prosperous and took an active part in the cultural and creative life of Germany. The hammer-like blow of the Nazis struck them unprepared.

Nothing like it had ever occurred in the history of the Jews. But there is a striking analogy almost four thousand years before that event. We are reading in Exodus (1:7-10) "And the children of Israel were fruitful, and increased abundantly, and multiplied, and waxed exceeding mighty; and the land was filled with them. Now there arose a new king over Egypt, which knew not Joseph. And he said unto his people, 'Behold, the people of the children of Israel are more and mightier than we. Come on, let us deal wisely with them, lest they multiply, and it come to pass, that, when there falleth out any war, they join also unto our enemies, and fight against us, and so get them up out of the land.' "

Now follows the story of the bondage of the Hebrews and their afflictions. The Egyptian taskmasters made the children of Israel serve "with rigor."

Pharaoh's edict to kill all male children is certainly less radical than Hitler's orders, but the organization of the ancient Egyptians was inferior to that of the Nazis.

Concerning the forced labor of Hebrews, it is interesting to compare it to the compulsory service into which the Jews were pressed in the beginning of the Nazi regime. The most cruel atrocities against them came later.

To the Hebrews in Egypt, as to the German Jews, the sudden change certainly was like a bolt from the blue, likewise destroying all their hopes and expectations. This reversal and heavy blow must be added to the many deep and overwhelming disappointments which the Hebrews suffered and which, later, also came under the power of the repetition compulsion.

At the moment we are interested in another aspect of this painful experience, namely, in its educational significance. Besides, the comparison with the individual will be helpful here. No child is born kind and considerate. Children are at first instinctively cruel and like to cause pain and suffering to others—not so much as an expression of their sadistic tendency but as manifestations of their power over persons and animals. Their education to kindness comes, as a matter of fact, late in the life of the child. Compassion is a late acquisition of childhood.

To give a typical example of the child's inconsiderateness:

A patient remembers—the recollection is confirmed by his mother—that as a little boy he once observed a maid ironing laundry and wanted her to do something strange. The girl happened to be ironing a piece of yellow linen, and the little boy asked her to iron out the canary that was loudly singing in its cage.

The education to compassion and to kindness is helped considerably when the child himself becomes subjected to suffering; that is, when he feels that others can inflict pain upon him. By this detour the child learns to appreciate and to experience pity.

The commandments of the Lord directed to the treatment of slaves and strangers, His forbidding to vex or to oppress them, are founded on that psychological consideration: "For ye were slaves in the land of Egypt." This was certainly more efficient and helpful than moralizing maxims. That unprecedented reform in the status of strangers and slaves was the more remarkable because it has no parallel in antiquity, when slavery was acknowledged as a normal institution.

Considering that the bondage of the ancient Hebrew tribes in Egypt was milder than the compulsory labor of the Jews in Germany, one comes to the surprising conclusion that the progress of mankind—if progress it is—moves in a way that makes a snail's pace seem like a forced march.

The Lost Mother-Goddess

It has become fashionable even among historians to glorify the qualities of the ancient Hebrews, to see them as being so different from other Amorite tribes and as forerunners of a higher civilization. They were nothing of the kind. They only became so, and only after going through a very hard school in which they had to suffer a great deal.

The absurd pride in Hebrew genealogy arouses less opposition than mirth. It brings to mind the humorous "Burlesque Biography" in which Mark Twain made fun of the grotesque worship of the family tree and of its pretensions.

Every reader of the Old Testament will encounter in it a gallery of criminals who commit worse misdeeds than did the imagined ancestors of the Mark Twain family in that humorous sketch. You will readily find fratricides, incestuous men, rogues, traitors, renegades. The ancient Hebrew tribes were at first no better than their neighbors. From a moralistic viewpoint they were actually worse, because these neighboring nations, especially the Egyptians and Babylonians, already had a fixed social organization, a highly developed code of law, and legislation that protected society from criminals. The half-barbaric Amorite tribes from which the Hebrews emerged had nothing comparable at their disposal.

Yet in one direction the ancient Hebrews soon became different from the neighboring nations whose civilization was superior to theirs. We are told that the Hebrew tribes soon began to worship a single invisible God. This cult, often discontinued and disturbed by the eruption of pagan rites, is assumed to have existed among the Hebrews from the time of Moses. This is, of course, incorrect. It was not until the period of the prophets that the monotheistic belief won out, if ever.[28]

From many indications one would suspect that a strong attraction to the cult of a female deity existed, since Astarte and other goddesses found so many worshipers even in later times.

Jewish religious teachers have tried to convince us that the ancient Hebrews were filled with loathing for the lasciviousness and obscenity of the religious ceremonies of other nations. The absence and the ban of a mother-goddess was often attributed to this instinctive hatred. Nothing could be more mistaken.

No doubt, the taboo of a mother-representative goddess figure has several determining causes, but the slow process of alienation was certainly due to the chief cause to which other factors later contributed. This primary cause was the relation to the soil, the land, and that early bitter disappointment produced by its aridity resulting in famine. We know that the traumatic experience forced the tribes to make their first migration. We know too that other ensuing famines necessitated further migrations. (Abraham's entrance into Egypt and the famine at the time of Joseph, mentioned in Genesis.)

The relation of a people to the soil is pattern forming in the same way that an individual is related to his mother. It is the mother who feeds the infant. Not only the sterility of the soil provided the incentive for the migration, but also the search for a new home, the longing for a more generous mother. The Hebrews daydreamed of Canaan, promised to them as a Lady Bountiful, as a country overflowing with milk and honey. Here was the picture of a freely giving foster-mother, of the "good earth" in contrast to the original land that had become parsimonious and mean.

The importance of this oral dependency, of alimentation, must also be highly valued in the life history of a people. When Moses led the children of Israel out of Egypt where they were cruelly oppressed and subjected to forced labor, they rebelled against him and Aaron in the wilderness of Sin. Again there was hunger (the repeated experience) and the children of Israel said unto them, "Would to God we had died by the hand of the Lord in the land of Egypt, when we sat by the flesh pots, and when we did eat bread to the full; for ye have brought us forth into this wilderness, to kill this whole assembly with hunger." (Exodus 16:3.)

They would have preferred to live as slaves having enough to eat rather than live as free men half-starving. On the other hand we find here a manifestation of a regressive trend and a longing for the lost country—also a recurrent phenomenon in Jewish history.

To return to our original theme: the bitter experience of that earliest period, the drying up of the soil of their original homeland, did not prevent those tribes from forming and worshiping the figure of a mother-goddess, but the repercussions of that primal experience led to an ambivalent attitude toward her, to an inherited vacillation between attraction and repulsion. This conflict of opposite forces resulted finally in the removal and the taboo of a mother-goddess.

Attraction and Repulsion

Perhaps the best way to illustrate the process just outlined is by comparing it with a little picture series I recently saw in a magazine. The first picture shows a mother and her little daughter walking together to the hospital. The little girl, holding her mother's hand, looks tenderly up at her mother. We then see the girl alone, lying in a hospital bed. Her gaze is fixed on the door of the room, anxiously awaiting the arrival of her mother—in vain. The child must stay in the hospital alone, and she seems to have lapsed into apathy. Finally her mother comes to get her daughter, who has now recovered. The last picture shows mother and daughter together again, walking to the exit of the hospital. But the attitude of the girl to mother is very different from the one seen in the first picture. The girl does not take her mother's hand, but walks a little distance from her; and she does not look up at her mother as before, but at her surroundings.

The comparison with this series of pictures will, I hope, clarify the far-reaching effects of the shocking experience to which the ancestors of the Israelites were subjected in that earliest phase. Their confidence in mother earth was diminished, as that first blind trust in the mother was shaken in the little girl. In the life of the little girl, Mother is still the most important person. She remains a godlike, powerful figure. Yet that unbounded confidence in her no longer exists. The ancestors of the Jews also cherished a mother-goddess figure and developed a cult about her. Yet, full reliance on her and on the country that had betrayed them could never again be regained. The later period is characterized by an ambivalent attitude toward her, by a longing for a mother-goddess and by a waning interest in her as a mother figure.

Again and again the mother-goddess has appeared in all her charm in the history of the children of Israel. We follow her periodic re-emergence from early biblical times, in which Astarte and Isis were worshiped by a renegade majority of Hebrews, up to the phase in which the Jewish colony in Egypt reintroduced her cult. We know that the lost or rather repressed figure of such a mother-goddess finally reappeared in the Virgin Mary in Christianity that came into the inheritance of the Hebrews.

Yet with the reintroduction of the mother-goddess the ties of the new religion with the old were dissolved. That break with the image of a mother-goddess for which the land was pattern-forming was absolute and irrevocable. There was no place for such a figure in official Judaism.

Even within the church that had inherited so much from the synagogue, the ancient image of the mother-goddess had undergone a radical transformation. The ancient mother figures of the Near East, Isis and Astarte as well as Aphrodite and Venus, were at the same time goddesses of love, or rather of sexual desire, and their cult was marked by the spirit of sexuality. Mary's figure is that of an untouched and untouchable virgin. The image of a goddess of love had already become intolerable and unacceptable for the renegade Jews who had become Christians.

The deepest reason for that change of character in the figure is, of course, the relationship with the divine-son figure whose ultimate nature is that of incest between mother and son.

The Repressed Son-God

All the ancient mother-goddesses of the Near East had their sons as lovers. There are Osiris, Attis, and Adonis, and other divine-son figures. The cult of the mother-goddess included, so to speak, the worship of her son and lover whose violent death was loudly and passionately lamented in the great festivals of ancient religions. With the removal of a mother-goddess the door was also closed to a son-god.

The Rabbi Jehoshuah of Nazareth could have been acceptable as a prophet to the Jews. Yes, he could even have been celebrated as a great man inspired by the Lord. But when he declared that he was the Son of God, when the legend of the virgin birth emerged, there was no longer any place for him within Jewish religion.[29]

Yet, at one time there was the figure of a divine son of God in the mythology of the Hebrew tribes. He was called Adam, and his mother was Eve, which means the Earth. It is easy to understand how this image of the son-god together with that of his divine mother was forever removed. You will recall the previously noted statement by Kadmi Cohen, that in primitive thinking the man is the male partner of the earth and the earth his mistress. Traces of the same conception are still found in the Adam story, but, as psychoanalysis has shown, in the mythology of all ancient people (for instance Gaea in Greek mythology), husbandry was originally regarded the same way.[30] The man who tills the ground is conceived of as having sexual intercourse with the land.

Returning once more to our original hypothesis, it can easily be guessed that early traumatic experience changed the position of the son-god figure, once worshiped by the ancient Hebrews as well as by the neighboring peoples. The great frustration and mortification those ancestors suffered when the desert took the place of fertile land, must have adversely affected their attitude to the son-god figure and in a profound way. The sexual frustration presented in that refusal of the earth was deeply felt, and the position of the son-god within the original mythology was seriously damaged. He was pushed into the background and his role finally became negligible. After many attempts to regain his rank, he disappeared in the substitute images of the Egyptian, Babylonian, and Greek son-gods.

Numerous attempts to reintroduce the image failed, but one finally succeeded. Jesus Christ took the vacant throne of the son-god who finally replaced the father-god. This figure thus marks the re-emergence of the original son-god whom the early ancestors of the Hebrew tribes had once known.

Only now, after a discussion of the removal of the mother-goddess and her divine son, can the far-reaching effects and repercussions of that early forgotten, but still unconquered, experience be evaluated.

The ancient Hebrews do not protest against their all-powerful God, but they sometimes solemnly object to the abuse of His power. Even some of the biblical figures enter a protest against decisions of Yahweh that seem to them too severe or unjust. Even in this early phase the Lord was sometimes embarrassingly contradicted.

Later, grievances against Him were frequently voiced.

The Jews sometimes became rebels with the greatest cause. The famous Rabbi Levi Yizchak of Berdichev stood before God and accused Him of being unjust to His people. The rabbi raised his hands to heaven in the synagogue, saying, "Father of the Universe, we will not let you do this to us any more. You have punished us more than we deserve." This is the voice of open rebellion speaking. It sounds quite different from Shylock's resignation.

> *Still have I borne it with a patient shrug;*
> *For sufferance is the badge of all our tribe. . . .*

The struggle of the Jews with God is similar to that in which the archangel Lucifer is engaged, though he was chosen by God as were the Jews. Lucifer, who is cast down into Hell and becomes Satan, continues his battle with God. In Milton's *Paradise Lost* Satan cries out against the Lord:

> *Then accursed by thy love for love or hate*
> *To me alike it deals eternal woe.*

Satan reappears as the champion of the rebellious Hebrews in the play *Jacob's Dream*, written by Richard Beer-Hofmann more than three hundred years after Milton. There also Satan proclaims that to be chosen by the Lord means to suffer. He sees the reverse side of being chosen and calls Jacob "God's chosen whipping boy." Jacob himself rebelliously asks:

"Why does He choose us and does not ask if we want to be chosen?"

The latter phase of the history of the ancient Hebrews, like that of the modern Jews, is filled with reports of continued open rebellion against their God.

As long as Yahweh was the God of His people, He was

bound to His narrow territory. When He became unlimited and illimitable, He became almost eliminated. It was less difficult to dismiss the Greek pantheon than the one and only God.

They used to tell a little story in Paris about Madame Geneviève Straus, the daughter of Halévy, composer of *La Juive*, who had a salon in the Rue Miromesnil. The noted Abbé Muquier, who had converted many Jews to Catholicism, tried to persuade Geneviève to join the Church, but she merely laughed and patted his hand, saying "Dear, dear Father, I have too little religion to risk changing what I've got." The majority of Western Jewish people, like this lady, have "too little religion" to be converted to Christianity. Also, in this sense the Jews are the "unreachables." The "death of God" that Nietzsche foresaw became a fact of contemporary civilization for the Jews also. The social function of religion has been reduced to such an extent that it is minimal and will disappear irretrievably. In this sense the fanaticism of some religious Jewish groups form a rear-guard action of belief.

The news of the demise of God has not yet reached some Jewish circles, but it will eventually be heard there too. No attempt to turn history back and to convert the Jews will succeed. In this direction, they will also remain "the unreachables."

The philosophers state that as a person is, so is his god, and add that if triangles were to have a god they would imagine him as being triangular.

Some Psychological Factors

Rudyard Kipling's saying, "There is something of the worst in the best of us and something of the best in the worst of us," has often been cited as a true psychological insight. Freud's statement, that the highest virtues we possess are unconsciously intimately connected with the things we most abhor, reaches a deeper level of psychological understanding. This insight was anticipated by Shakespeare when he wrote:

> *They say best men are moulded out of faults.*
> *And, for the most, become much more the better*
> *For being a little bad.*

The preceding paragraph was meant to bring some additional psychological factors into the discussion of the problems dealt with here. In *Beyond the Pleasure Principle* Freud explicitly states that the dominance of the compulsion to repeat does not preclude the fact that certain character traits also contribute to the working-out of individual destiny. There is ample room left for the dynamic influence of characterological elements.

Are any such distinguishing traits recognizable in the history of the Jews? An understanding of them would lead to a valuable contribution to gaining a grasp of the nature of the Jewish group character.

In a little book that analyzes the peculiarities of Jewish

wit, I have already made one attempt at this goal.[31] This attempt was only partially successful, and the validity of its results is restricted to a definite, narrow sphere. Nevertheless, one of the points made in that book can be repeated here, namely, that an oscillation between a masochistic and a paranoid attitude is discernible in the character of the ancient Hebrews. In the preceding paragraphs these two attitudes were dealt with only with regard to God, but their effects extend far beyond the religious sphere. The essential difference between them, characterized by Jule Nydes, is as follows: "The masochist appears to renounce power for the sake of power." In this formulation the word "appears" must be well considered because both types wish to become powerful.

The masochistic character tries to win love and protection through suffering and submission, but he too wants to force the superior person to serve him. It is further to be considered that both dynamics often appear in combination.

At this point caution is well advised. In stating that an oscillation between masochistic and paranoid attitudes can be observed in the Jewish character, we must add that it is a question of two opposing tendencies which frequently appear but need not always become actualized. Also, it cannot be said that the same or similar tendencies are absent in the character of other groups. It is more a matter of intensity or quantity than of presence or absence.

With these preliminary remarks in mind, it is significant to note that the Hebrews as well as their descendants had no power. In the majority of historic situations which we can follow, they try to attain their aims only by submission and compliance, by bowing and scraping—in short, by a masochistic attitude.

This was as true in their relation to God as in their attitude toward the secular authority of the countries they lived in. They were dependent on the pity and protection granted them by both. An effective way to gain their ends was the demonstration, or rather the display, of their miserable and poor situation. Often along with that display was a petition to God in which deep remorse was expressed. One's own sinfulness was emphasized and forgiveness was asked. The Jews plead with their God and the secular authorities for protection and other favors—simply because they had confessed their moral weakness. Their humility was a valuable weapon in their struggle for power.

Yet when they had acquired power and influence, their humility began to disappear. They began to entertain ideas of grandeur and superiority, and they considered themselves "exceptions." In this connection Freud's remarks on the type of exceptions are apropos. He treated some patients who claimed to be exempt from the rules and regulations that bound everybody else. Freud found analogous behavior in the life of groups, referring to the attitude of a whole people whose past is fraught with suffering. In that Jewish claim to being exceptions we at once recognize the paranoid character. Jule Nydes considers it significant that the Jews in their wanderings never entered foreign lands as menials or as peasants. From the very outset their aspiration was to establish a relationship with the authorities of that land. Upon reaching the position they want, the illusion of being the chosen people of God is maintained. "Unhappily, however, such a situation made them the ideal scapegoat," Jule Nydes remarks.[32] Once again we arrive at that indelible track, the repetition compulsion.

I know, of course, that the characteristic features presented here are only temporary, determined by the conditions in which the Jews have lived. Yet those features can be seen far back in the course of history.

A whole series of fascinating psychological and sociological questions emerges at this point, but I am unable to solve them. It is a hurdle I cannot jump.

From the Letter of an Unknown Woman

What follows is a kind of appendage to the preceding paragraphs. The Jews have been held responsible for most of the evils in the world, from the crucifixion of Christ in antiquity, the plagues in medieval times, to international and social conflicts in our time. They were accused of every crime conceivable. It was as if they had opened a Pandora's box from which all sorts of evil were let loose into the world. Grievances against them include such contradictory statements as that they laid the foundations both of capitalism and of communism.

Yet there are—will wonders never cease?—still to be heard some original thoughts of this kind. The other day I heard a man discussing the Nazi period and he called the Jews "injustice collectors." Not many of the accusations are as bizarre as that catch phrase. Take the following case:

A gentile woman, a writer, sent me some fan letters about my biblical tetralogy and expressed great interest in further studies concerning the prehistory of the Jews. I quote from a letter of hers discussing the national characteristics of those ancient people: ". . . and now, I'm wondering if it might not be true to say that the Hebrews were basically lazy—in that they would rather argue out points of philosophy or the right way to run their community down to the last jot and tittle, and that they regarded hard physical work as inferior. They, the thinkers, should be above labors. . . . Could we not make such a sweeping statement —that, if you divide people into the thinkers and the doers, the Jews were surely in the first group, looked down on in the second, and because of this . . . usually ended up with nothing? . . . Which brings me to my second thought; I had put it to myself as a question: Babylon—Troy—Greek —Roman civilization—all have perished. Why has the Jew alone survived? Could it be because he expected nothing?

"If you build your hopes on a multitude of material objects, you can lose it all. If you have nothing to start with except the ability to reproduce your own kind, why—what have you got to lose . . . ? I leave the answer in your expert hands."

I do not know all the answers. I do not even know all questions. We shall return later to the question of the great or little expectations of the Jews. At this point I am only interested in the surprising suggestion that the Hebrews were a lazy people. It is hardly possible that my correspondent meant the ancient Hebrews. Perhaps she had in mind the ghetto Jews of later times when she stated that they were busy with their religious philosophy (does she mean Talmud study?) and with running their community (rather, their congregation?) instead of doing hard physical labor.

I know of no evidence to confirm the belief that the Jews regarded physical work as inferior. It is, of course, very easy to state that the Hebrews did not belong to the doers but to the thinkers; but, as de Gaulle recently said, the comfortable way is rarely the right one. No facts in their history testify in favor of the opinion that the Hebrews were lazy. The only fact arguing for this statement is its originality. Is it correct to say that the Jews shunned hard physical labor?

The dockyard laborers of Saloniki in Greece were all Jews, as are many workers in every country. A recent study in New York showed that this city, from which the great Jewish labor movement arose, still has large numbers of Jewish workers: garment workers, painters, carpenters, glaziers, waiters, barbers, taxidrivers, and so on. The commentator states that the tone of New York as a "Jewish" city is communicated to visitors as much by workers as by businessmen and professionals. According to this study (in 1952), manual workers made up a third of Jewish employed males.[33]

There is, however, one kind of manual work which has occupied very few Jewish people, namely, farming. It can, of course, be argued that at certain periods rural areas were forbidden to the Jews and that they were pulled into urban life because it was only there that they could find employment and a living.[34] One might add that only the possessor of the soil is dedicated to farmwork and likes to till the soil. Yet all this does not explain the peculiar turning away from agriculture found among the Jews. It must have deep-lying roots.

It is true that the Hebrews in Canaan were farmers too, although the majority were shepherds.[35] The pioneers in modern Israel tilled the soil of the country they considered their own with at least the same zeal as the farmer of other countries. Yet it is true that for almost two thousand years Jews have avoided agricultural work.

If the hypothesis previously set forth is correct, there has been, so to speak, among Jews a kind of inherited aversion to farming. When the soil of the Jews' original home dried up, when that fertile land became desert, it had, as it were, betrayed, frustrated, and deceived their ancestors. The traces of that disappointment are still evident in much later times. The Hebrews turned to work on the soil in

Canaan, but they took up farming in the way a child becomes fond of a foster mother, the substitute of his real mother. The impression of that early experience has not been obliterated, merely repressed. The later events, of being driven out of Canaan and the dispersion that followed, only intensified the earlier impression and reopened the old wound. It is remarkable that agriculture is a favored occupation to the Israelis who returned to their homeland.

The Jewish aversion to agriculture can be readily compared with another phenomenon that is more familiar to us. We know that there have been very few eminent Jewish painters and sculptors during the past two thousand years. It has been only in the last two centuries, and more particularly in the last hundred years, that Jews have distinguished themselves as painters (Jozef Israels, Chagall, and others), and sculptors (Epstein and others). The reason for the absence of accomplished Jewish artists is, of course, determined by the effect of the biblical interdiction against making graven images of things and persons. The continued effect of that injunction produced an avoidance among Jews in using their artistic talents.

Similarly, an aversion to agricultural work was the result of early conditioning. Not divine prohibition, but the repressed memory of the Jewish people is to blame for their avoidance of the soil that had cruelly and woefully disappointed them. Here is the Ariadne thread to guide us from that labyrinth of problems back to prehistory. Other motives, no doubt, helped produce that avoidance, but the original traumatic experience had, so to speak, gotten under their skin. In all of us our ancestors continue to live; they continue their thwarted and deprived existence. The experiences of the forefathers thus unconsciously influence the life of their descendants. Victor Hugo once said that the dead are not absent, but only invisible.

Figure of the Future

Introduction

My telescopic account of Jewish history has surely done violence to the richness of the subject. My major concern has been to examine afresh an aspect of Jewish history that had escaped the observation of the historians.

The third part of this book is of a different character from the preceding ones. I was tempted to call it "Another Part of the Forest," but was disturbed by the thought that in our present civilization it would be more justly described as "another part of the jungle."

Until now we have occupied ourselves with ideas about the unconquered past, with what the Germans call the "*unbewältigte Vergangenheit.*" We were absorbed in conjectures about the prehistory of the Hebrews based on a hypothesis and on the deplorably scarce information available. There were an abundance of problems to come to grips with. But now, when we turn to the present and to the future the material becomes altogether problematical. The historian Michelet lectured to his class on July 27, 1830, while cannon fire erupted in the streets of Paris. Michelet said to his students: "Gentlemen, they are making history; we shall write it." But did the historian and his students describe the events correctly? This is very doubtful. Only recently we heard the violent and noisy discussion centered upon the book *Eichmann in Jerusalem* by Hannah Arendt who was an eye-witness to the events she described yet whose statements were fiercely contested.

In any case it is necessary to turn our attention to present events, if we want to record its history. Then we shall try to guess what the future might be. The study of the past will help us because one must go back before he can go forward.

What is the situation of the Jews in the world today? What was undertaken, what attempt was made to save them from their fatal and malignant repetition compulsion?

It is true that the Catholic Church has, at least officially, abandoned her persecution, as have other denominations. But there are other, no less poisonous arguments advanced against the Jews: economic, racial, and psychological objections are arrayed against the position of the Jews in various countries.[36] But let us rather turn to those nations, countries, or programs that promise a solution to the Jewish question, which is rather an intricate knot of questions, difficult to disentangle.

The United States

A memory intrudes when I try to describe the situation in America, "an island of freedom in the world," as a commentator recently called it. I am not sure of the date, but it was many years before the Nazis came to Austria and it was in midsummer. Sinclair Lewis and Dorothy Thompson visited Freud on the Semmering, a summer resort in the mountains, a few hours' train ride from Vienna. We, too, were spending the summer there, in the Südbahnhotel, close by Freud's cottage, and he invited me over. We had an extremely entertaining evening. Sinclair Lewis was in a very good mood and we laughed a lot.

This was, of course, years before he wrote that novel *It Can't Happen Here,* and no one thought it could happen in Austria. I recalled that evening on the Semmering when I spent my first summer in the United States, a refugee from Hitler. At last, in democratic America, I felt I was free from the burden of European race hatred and discrimination.

On the first occasion when I received a negative answer from a mountain hotel where we wanted to stay for the summer, I was merely astonished, but then I received similar letters of refusal from other hotels. I was taken aback and alarmed. The letters were always polite but definite, and I finally asked one hotel management why we were not accepted as guests. I was told that the hotel, "to its greatest regret," accepted no Jewish guests because other long-standing clients would object.

Two years later we were at Lake Placid. In this beautiful place the country club did not allow Jews on the premises. I could enumerate many instances of discrimination against Jews I have met with during the twenty-six years that the United States has been my domicile. But what's the use? This country is a melting pot of all nations, and all Americans are immigrants or descendants of immigrants. Yet the melting pot does not simmer well.

Recently the neo-Nazis held a parade in the heart of New York. The Birch Society and the Ku Klux Klan still proclaim that Jews have no place in the United States. The news-

papers of today report continuing discrimination against
Jews who seek apartments in New York's upper East Side.
The Constitution still protects Jews, but how long will this
protection be granted to them? Can't it happen here? Perhaps not in the next few years, but some day in the foreseeable future it can happen here in America, which is not
only our country but also belongs to our children and grandchildren.

Communism

In certain respects the Jew Karl Marx was anti-Semitic. In
his article on the Jewish question Marx, then twenty-five,
accused the Jews of introducing capitalism and of exploiting
the poor.[37] Is it in consequence or in continuation of those
thoughts that the communistic states which proclaim
themselves followers of Marx's program are anti-Semitic?
However, what interests us here is the compulsion to repeat
in the destiny of the Jews under a communistic regime, in
a new milieu. Jews played a prominent part in the Russian
revolutionary movement and some (Trotzky) reached high
positions. At first Russian Jewry experienced a cultural
flowering. The emancipation of nationalities in the cultural
sphere was favorable to the Yiddish language and schools.
The Jewish theater and newspapers developed and flourished under the new regime.

When Stalin died in 1953, all this changed. Yiddish

literature was suppressed, Jewish writers were expelled, and the Jewish physicians who had treated Stalin were accused of murder. It was clear that all this, especially the turn against Zionism, was the beginning of a sharp anti-Jewish attitude which became more and more pronounced. There were no longer Jewish schools, newspapers, or publishing houses in the Soviet Union. The old pattern had repeated itself. The Jews were welcomed at first, sometimes became leaders of the new ideas, then the anti-Jewish tendency grew until the Jews were systematically suppressed. It should not be surprising that this tendency increased by leaps and bounds and was turned against Zionism as well as against Judaism.

The Russian atheists were no less intolerant toward religious than the Church was toward godlessness. The lot of the Jews under the communistic regime was almost as unhappy as under the Czarist tyranny. There are, strangely enough, people who maintain that one must also be tolerant towards intolerance.

Israel

Is there no exit? The other avenue that promised a salvation from the repetition compulsion bears the name of Zionism. Almost everyone—that is, all *hommes de bonne volonté*—will welcome the creation of Palestine as a haven of refuge for the numberless persecuted people from all over the world and as a philanthropic shelter for the poor and aged Jews. Everyone without exception will applaud the enthusiasm and the work of the Jewish pioneers and the defenders of the old-new country. Welcome and praise for Israel does not, however, prevent us from asking how long its existence can last. When I was in Palestine in 1937, I experienced an Arab attack upon our car as we drove along the serpentine road from Tel-Aviv to Jerusalem. Fortunately, such attacks are no longer possible, or rather are now only possible in the frontier region of the new state. Yet, encircled by deeply hostile nations whose greatest wish is to drive all the Jews of Palestine into the sea, how long can a national homeland exist?

Without considering such realistic and practical things, is a national homeland for the Jews desirable? Would it really put an end to the Diaspora? In a recent discussion of the Galuth, Alfred Kazin remarked, "I would feel exiled in Israel too." [38]

Should all the suffering of the Jewish people through two millennia really end in their becoming a nation like any other, in having a flag, a national emblem, and a small territory of their own? Is this the aim, the vision the prophets had foreseen?

Decidedly not. The country of the Jews must be larger. It must be as wide as the earth. They will not be citizens of a certain state, but citizens of the world. Citizens of a future which does not know states or nationalities, does not acknowledge races and colors. All the forces now at work are pressing in the direction of a United Mankind.

Someone called the Jews "God's experiment with man." Should the experiment He had formed in His mind have failed? If the Jews would become a nation like any other, it would mean the failure of their mission as the religious people would call it. The failure of their function as we would put it.

Will the identity of the Jews still be maintained then? Perhaps so, but only in the sense of members of a family, of a group that belong to the family of Man.

There are many kinds of problems which should be discussed here, but some questions have to be answered before we turn to them.

A Glance at Anti-Semitism

Dr. Paul Federn, our late colleague, who died in 1950, when asked, "How are you?" used to answer, "That does not concern me." Jews might answer in a similar vein to the question of anti-Semitism as a general problem. It does not concern them. It is not their problem but that of other groups. The solution of this problem does not depend on the behavior of the Jews, nor on their situation in various countries.

The subject itself cannot be disregarded because anti-Semitism in one of the strongest forces that keeps alive the compulsion to repeat in Jewish history. Yet the subject can only be skirted here with a few incidental remarks. My casual comments are not intended as an addition to the immense literature of Jew hatred. The interest expressed is in itself a manifestation of attention which should be flattering to the Jews in a certain sense, as if they were something special.

What is anti-Semitism? Sholem Asch asserts that it is not a movement, but a disease.[39] "He who is infected by it is unable to have an orientation, a judgment or an opinion which is the result of logical thinking or of authentic facts." The anti-Semite has, Asch says, "no proof, no opinion, no consciousness even, because proof, opinion and consciousness are attained through independent thought. He has no independent thought; he is imprisoned within the magic circle in which his sufferings have immured him."

Is anti-Semitism, whose program is to free the world from the sickness of Judaism, a disease? This is the place to quote, "Physician, heal thyself." If, on the other hand, to be a Jew is a disease, then it is congenital and no cure for it is known. Some people say that anti-Semitism is the universal example of xenophobia—hatred and fear of foreigners. As Nikolai Berdyaev declared, it would be "a primitive dislike of the Jews as representing a group which is different, unfamiliar and strange." [40] The primary cause of hostility toward Jews would be this quality of "otherness."

This Russian philosopher Nikolai Berdyaev (1874-1948), in condemning anti-Semitism, argues that the inferior Jewish race is also considered to be the strongest, eternally triumphant over all the others, wherever free competition exists. Confronted with this irreconcilable condition, he protests that, after all, "one can't surrender everything to the Jews." They have made all the scientific discoveries, distinguished themselves as eminent philosophers, founded capitalist industry, recruited the world socialist movement, and concentrated public opinion and the press into their hands. "I avow," says he, "that as an Aryan my self-respect is wounded and I refuse to accept this point of view."

Can one still discuss racial anti-Semitism? We have

known for a long time that it is not based upon science, but upon mythology, fairy tales pretending to the scientific truths.

And what if hatred of the Jews stems from religious motives? A single voice, that of the ardent French Catholic philosopher Leon Bloy (1840-1917) should be heard on this subject. [41] "Suppose that there were people around you continually speaking of your father and mother with the utmost contempt, who had nothing to offer them but insults and offensive sarcasm, how would you feel? Well, this is just what happens to our world of Jesus Christ."

People have forgotten, or rather do not want to know, that Christ was a Jew, his mother a Jewess, that the Apostles were Jews, and that the whole liturgy of the Church is drawn from Jewish books. Bloy's work, *Vieux de la Montagne,* which thus exposes the outrage and blasphemy of vilifying the Jews, contains the striking sentence: "Anti-Semitism . . . is the most horrible slap in the face suffered in the ever-continuing passion of our Lord."

Enough, perhaps even too much, has been said about the meaning of anti-Semitism. However you twist and turn the question, it remains a problem of the gentile nations. It is not ours—not a Jewish problem.

The Survival Miracle

There is a single problem with which we have not yet come to grips, that of the survival of the Jews. It has occupied the thought of many people in the past and will no doubt occupy more enlightened minds in the future. It was called to mind again by that woman's letter, quoted earlier, in which she asked herself if the Jews had not survived so many ancient civilizations simply because they had not expected anything.

Yet the survival miracle is as old as the existence of the Hebrews, and is subjected to the repetition-compulsion just as are their vicissitudes. It is more than accidental that it is anticipated in that wonderful sentence: "The bush burned with fire, and the bush was not consumed" (Exodus 3:2). It seems to me that the bush burning with fire but remaining unconsumed is not evidence of the angel of the Lord, but conjures up a vision of the Hebrew future.

Only a short-sighted and superficial view will see a promise of personal longevity in the commandment, "Honor thy father and thy mother, that thy day may be long upon the land which the Lord thy God giveth thee." I am convinced that the commandment promises a long life of the generations, the survival of the Hebrew tribes.

In the following pages a new approach to the old problem is attempted, an approach so novel that many will call it a tour de force and some even a tour de farce.

The turtle cannot move forward if it does not stick its neck out. My neck has been stuck out so far that if I extended it further I would resemble a giraffe rather than a turtle. Yet I want to continue along the path that beckoned me, if only to see where it leads.

This new approach is characterized by an analogy or similarity in function with other theories. The road we shall travel diverges widely from others, but in a sense it runs parallel to certain observations in biological laboratories and must not be misunderstood. It is only a comparison meant to illustrate a process which is difficult to describe and to present to unprepared readers.

The observations and experiments alluded to were made during the early part of this century. I have not followed the later literature and do not know whether the results of recent research have invalidated or qualified the earlier findings.

Those experiments, presented in simplest, nontechnical terms, concern the duration life for generations of protozoa, one-celled animals. The American Woodruff experimented with paramecium, or "slipper animalcule," which is a ciliate, a microscopic animal living in water. The paramecium reproduces by fission into two individuals. Woodruff isolated one individual after each fission and placed it in new water. He continued the experiment until the 3,029th generation. This last descendant was as lively as its remote ancestor, showing no sign of old age nor any willingness to die. It seemed that under favorable conditions these microscopic animals were actually immortal.

The experiments of other biologists led to different results. Maupas, Calkins and others arrived at the experimental conclusion that the paramecium, after a certain number of divisions, diminishes in size, become weaker, loses some part of their organization, and finally die. There are, however, certain measures that can postpone the senescence and death of the protozoa. They become, so to speak, rejuvenated when they conjugate, an act corresponding to sexual reproduction in later phases of evolution. In this act of conjugation two individuals interchange their substance.

The same rejuvenating results are obtained by introducing agents which have a stimulating effect, for instance by changing the fluid in which those microscopic animals exist, by raising their temperatures, and even by shaking them.

Woodruff's experiments were not conclusive because he provided each generation with fresh, nourishing fluid. He was thus led to the conclusion that the protozoa become old because they expel the products of their own metabolism into the surrounding water. Only the products of their own metabolism had this injurious effect. The same paramecia that were subjected to the fatal consequences of their own metabolism did not perish, but flourished in a fluid containing the waste products of a species only distantly related to them.

It is time to return to our major theme. The new approach previously mentioned is essentially a comparison of the survival conditions of the Jews with those of the protozoa.

I am afraid that at this point most readers will vigorously protest against such a comparison. What, they will say, is the sense of comparing the life of a protozoa, the most primitive single-celled animal, with that of whole groups of highly organized human beings?

As we have said, the analogy is meant as an illustration. All the objections that can be anticipated need not prevent us from continuing to use the biological analogy to illustrate a social process within a certain group. The question is, if the life of protozoa can be prolonged, or their senescence and death postponed, by change in their nutrient fluid, is it not then imaginable that the life duration of groups could also be extended when they are put into a new milieu, an environment very different from their previous one?

Biologists think that the animalcules perish because of the waste products of their own metabolism, but they gain a new lease on life, so to speak, when they are transported into the nutrient fluid of another species. Would it be too bold to speculate that groups also, when brought into different national and cultural environments, could similarly obtain a new lease on life?

Is it too daring to surmise that the Jews, who repeatedly found themselves in new countries and alien civilizations, were restored and somehow renewed by contact with a different cultural milieu?

There is no doubt that they were dispersed over the whole world, living in the Greek, Roman, Persian, Spanish, and German countries until they were again expelled and took refuge in other lands. Is that lease on life perhaps the effect of their dispersion? Is their miraculous longevity with respect to many ancient civilizations a result of their dispersion?

I raise the question but do not answer it; yet I believe that the Jews would have perished had they continued to live in Palestine for two thousand years. That is to say, their lot would have been the same as that of the Greeks, the Romans, and the Babylonians. I believe that the Diaspora, or the exile which the Jews call Galuth, does not have the character of a haunting curse, but of a blessing in disguise. Am I "a dreamer of dreams" to believe this?

I know, of course, how heretic such a view must sound to the religious as well as to Zionist Jews, but some biological and psychological considerations would speak for its truth. It gives me some consolation in my isolated position that quite a few Jewish mystics have expressed opinions similar to mine.

Theories like this, because they are not founded on substantial evidence, give the impression of being distressingly venturesome. Sometimes a shot in the dark will hit the target, too.

The Nature of Dispersion

Some serious questions confront us at this point, the most important being that of the significance of the unique phenomenon, the Diaspora. Also, this problem has been studied and overstudied until the traditional modes of expression about it are worn out. That part of Jewish history is too important to leave to the historians.

We should dare to approach it from a novel side. As the avant garde of future researchers we dare to question anew the meaning of the Jewish dispersion. The most practical approach is to avail ourselves of some observations made in clinical psychoanalysis. Numerous experiences have led to the conclusion that from the effect of a certain behavior pattern of an individual one can reason out his motive or at least one of his dominant conscious or unconscious motives. This is quite obvious and easy to understand when that behavior is in the interest of the individual. Let us take for instance the case of a young man looking for a job as a clerk. When he applies, he will, of course, try to show his abilities and qualifications to the best advantage. But what would one think if the applicant's behavior shows just the opposite? What if he emphasized his lack of experience, the fact that he is unable to type, that he has not learned this or that skill? In short, what if he demonstrated that he could not be employed although he wished very much to obtain the job?

Does such paradoxical behavior justify the conclusion

that its effect reveals a determining motive? May we still think that the young man, in spite of his conscious wishes, wants to fail in his application? Yes, that conclusion is indeed psychologically permissible, especially when we consider that there are unconscious self-sabotaging or masochistic tendencies at work in the young man. Such considerations of the unconscious or repressed agencies make it possible to explain the apparently unreasonable attitude of some people.

One might be able to transfer the results of those clinical cases to the sphere of group psychology. Here, too, it is valid to reach a conclusion from the effect of a certain behavior pattern to the motives behind it. Is it not then possible to imagine that the dispersion of the Jews over the world also had an unconscious function or that it reflects certain hidden tendencies?

What can be said about the unconscious motives and effects of the dispersion? No doubt they originated as a continuation of that first Hebrew emigration from their primal home in north Arabia when that fertile country became an ocean of sand. The migrations are still in the service of the repetition compulsion. Yet they acquired a new function as the ancient urge, the search for pastures, continued in a modern form. The new function was that everywhere the Jews came they disseminated and propagated—in Christendom and in Islam—conveying their message of social justice. The Jews were oppressed, tortured, driven out, yet their message persisted and worked beneath the surface.

Besides this function there was another that became manifest by the Jews' very existence, and by the contributions they made to the civilization of every country in which they remained for a long time. They fructified this alien civilization by their work, served as translators and transmitters of other languages and literatures, and transfused, so to speak, the blood of their own civilization into the veins of the people who were their hosts.

In this sense they form a binding force par excellence because they joined with and united the people of various countries. They linked them together in a union of nations which reaches far beyond the formal corporation that was called the League of Nations (even that idea originates in the utterances of the Hebrew prophets).

The unconscious meaning of the Diaspora is thus the tying together of people in the spirit of social justice, valid for all. The Jews have no country of their own. Their country is the earth. They are in a sense not citizens of any state, but citizens of a world to come.

All this is, of course, music of the future, but it is distinctly audible when one listens with the third ear to the symphony of Jewish history and follows its leitmotif, which is the expression of the repetition compulsion at work within it.

Right or wrong, I see no other meaning or unconscious significance in the migrations and the dispersion of the Jews which are their unique destiny. Otherwise it seems to be a wandering that leads nowhere.

Recently Gershom Scholem, professor of the Hebrew University in Jerusalem and the famous author of *Major Trends in Jewish Mysticism* wrote: "I am aware that there are aspects of Jewish history (and for more than forty years I have concerned myself with little else) which are beyond our comprehension." [42] It is very possible that the Diaspora belongs to those impenetrable problems or, to put it more cautiously, to those that are at present still inscrutable.

Repetition and Resistance

The more one looks into the past, the farther one can see into the future. This is also true for the sphere with which this essay is concerned. We followed the repetition compulsion in its effect throughout Jewish history, a history which is the same story always. The Jews come into a foreign country, are sometimes welcomed there, and distinguish themselves in many professions and offices. They arouse the envy of people who incite the mob against them. A secret storm is stirred up. Persecutions set in, massacres and riots follow. The end is expulsion, flight, or annihilation.

But if this embodies the character of repetition compulsion, how can we reconcile such tremendous suffering and such a cruel fate with an unconscious motive of uniting all people? There is certainly a contradiction—unless we assume that their aim must be achieved precisely through or in spite of any oppression. It is as if they constitute a living warning and a historic reminder.

But setting aside for the moment of such improbable considerations, it must be assumed that the repetition compulsion presents an almost insurmountable obstacle to the attainment of that unconscious aim. It works, as we know, beyond the pleasure principle and strives to conquer age-old traumatic experiences of the people. In this function it stubbornly resists the effort to fulfill those secret tendencies. Resistance to them exists not only in the minds and hearts of the host nations, but also within the Jews themselves, who try to master the sorrowful past that has left indelible traces on their character. It would appear that all hope in the Jewish question is founded on overcoming the compulsion to repeat.

Perhaps the alternative would be if even this compulsion could finally be put into the service of those hidden tendencies. This may not be probable, but it does have a certain compelling illogic.

The Lord says, "Behold, I have refined thee, but not with silver; I have chosen thee in the furnace of affliction (Isaiah 48:10). Why the Lord chose them remains a mystery. The ways of the Lord are mysterious, and, as Freud once casually remarked, rarely pleasant.

But Freud was an uncompromising atheist. Perhaps the Talmud knows better. It asks, "Why is Israel compared to an olive tree?" and answers, "Because just as an olive yields its best only when pounded, so is Israel at its best under oppression."

The Will to Live

In following the idea of a repetition compulsion Freud arrived at a new conception of the nature of instinct, namely, at a dualistic theory in which there are contrasting life-and-death instincts. Without entering into a discussion of these abstract speculations, it must be said that in this hypothesis the life-preserving instincts stand in marked opposition to

the idea that all instinctual life serves to bring about death
or a return to an inorganic existence.

One of the many functions of the self-preserving instinct
is the assurance that "the organism shall follow its own path
to death. The organism thus wishes to die only in his own
fashion." The organism struggles most energetically against
dangers and other events which might accelerate death by
a kind of short circuit.[43]

This is, of course, not entirely correct and should be qualified, but its partial imminent truth leads to a related problem which it is now necessary to discuss.

I am not concerned here with the theory of life-and-death
instincts nor with any abstract speculations, but with a fact
known to physicians, psychologists, priests, and others. I
mean the will to live and the readiness to die or, rather, the
acquiescence to death. All observers agree that this conscious or unconscious factor is one of the agencies that influence the course of a serious illness or the outcome of a
dangerous situation.

This special phenomenon is an adjournment or delay in
dying; it is, so to speak, the timing of one's own death.

A few examples will illustrate that respite. A woman who
for many years had suffered from a dangerous heart ailment
was overcome by an attack on the train ride from Palestine
to Vienna where her parents lived. At that time the journey
lasted many days and nights and during it she suffered considerable pain. Upon arrival in Vienna, she was brought to
her parents' home by ambulance and died a few minutes
after seeing them. An old writer who suffered from advanced
arteriosclerosis made a kind of vow to himself that he would
not die until he had completed a book he was working on.
He died a few hours after dictating the closing sentences. A
clerk whose days were numbered wanted to live long enough
so that his widow would be entitled to receive a government

pension. He desperately endured the cancer that doomed him until the anticipated date. The man died the morning after the pension went into effect.

Thus the will to live until a certain date fights successfully against the powers that drive the individual to his death. The all-important dates in these instances are clearly tied up with the fulfillment of an urgent and dominant wish, a wish to finish a manuscript, to see one's parents again, to secure a pension for a surviving wife. The hour of dying is, so to speak, postponed until the necessary circumstances for that wish fulfillment are present or the wish is realized. The reprieve was, of course, only temporary, but it accomplished the desired results.

Am I being too bold to assume that a similar unconscious will to live also operates in groups or nations and that it determines their survival and time of death? We know that certain species of animals—for instance the dinosaur—vanished because they could not adapt themselves to their environment. Other animals with greater adaptability could survive great changes of temperature, and other factors. This seems to me to offer a palpable analogy to the migratory tendencies of the Jews who, upon coming into a new milieu, have tried to adapt themselves.

Psychological as well as biological considerations of a collective will to live would allow us to assume that the Jewish people, like the individuals mentioned, are unconsciously determined to live and not to give up their identity until their social function is fulfilled. (I have intentionally avoided the theological expression of a mission in which I do not believe.)

What is that collective, unconsciously pursued life purpose? We have tried to answer that question, and only want to add that this function is also determined by well-known factors. The destiny of an individual is the result of two vital agencies. It is determined by what the individual brings with him into life—his heritage, and what life brings to him —his vicissitudes. What is his inheritance? It is the result of the lives of his ancestors. In the last analysis it is the consequence of the climate, of the country in which they have lived, of its fauna and flora, of its soil.

Once again we are led back to that early traumatic event in Hebrew prehistory, that experience which the Hebrews tried to master emotionally in their repetition compulsion.

Other later experiences also left indelible traces on the character, the aspirations, and the particular objects in view unconsciously established by the Hebrews. They are contained in the reminders: "Because thou wert slaves in the land of Egypt."

A Few Questions

The Jews must, we have said, fulfill certain functions until they too are submerged in the conglomeration of all people. Of course, these functions are also determined by the qualities and faults, the positive and negative characteristics of the people who fulfill them. The peculiar gifts and lack of other qualities in a people play a decisive part in this. It cannot be accidental that the Greeks produced wonderful works of art and that the Romans were masters in the sphere of law and political organization.

The sublime aim of uniting people and promoting equality

among them does not exclude, but rather includes the co-operation of some elementary drives. In the case of the Jews there must have been an unconscious urgent wish to be loved and acknowledged, a kind of sublimated love of mankind, and its counterforce.

It is one of the greatest ironies of world history that the very people who so passionately wanted to be loved and admired became perhaps the most hated. The attempt to answer the question of how this came about would lead us too far afield.

Other questions are easier to grapple with; for instance, why a state of affairs such as the one we have predicted has not been realized before? The answer is: It was too early— too early for the gentiles as it was for the Jews, although it was not too early to foresee the situation. The Hebrew prophets foretold it and Mohammed proclaimed in the Koran: "All nations are a single nation."

In 1627 Sir Francis Bacon's *New Atlantis* described airplanes, submarines, and sound-carrying devices. He predicted the telephone two hundred and fifty years before it was invented. In 1894 John Jacob Astor's *A Journey in Other Worlds* described television—picture telephones. In 1638 Francis Godwin wrote *Man in the Moone*, in which the moon's lesser gravitational attraction is envisioned.

The future evolution of mankind, including general disarmament and the disappearance of national barriers, was much easier to foresee than technological devices.

We psychoanalysts know how slow is the progress of characterological change and how long it takes to bring about emotional modifications. Obviously it will take even longer to produce changes in the intellectual and emotional attitudes of the masses. We must consider that only a very short time has passed since mankind worshiped fetishes, saw God in a stone or plant, practiced cannibalism. How short a time has passed since man has outgrown his crudest barbarism! Comparatively speaking, mankind is still in its infancy and the Neanderthaler is our contemporary.

This brings us to another point. The future as it has been envisioned here will certainly bring its conflicts and discords among various groups and individuals. What is foreseen here is only an improvement in human relations, a step toward humanization of man, not a radical change. Perfection cannot be expected because there is nothing perfect on this earth, nor in heaven.

Conclusion

There are a few obstacles that must be removed before we can shut the door on this essay. At this point it is worth a little trouble and time to return to the subject of the life story of the protozoa. Biologists have learned how those one-celled animals can attain a new lease on life under the influence of chemical or even mechanical changes, for instance, when their nutrient fluid is changed or even when they were disturbed. An analogy between this prolongation of individual protozoan life and the duration of the Jewish people was then offered. The Jews were, so to speak, kept alive by their migrations and by their repeated transplantation into different cultures. In this way, they became the nearest thing to an "eternal people."

Yet there is no such thing as an eternal people, any more

than an eternal individual. We all owe nature our death. In the realm of the protozoa too, that new lease on life is not equivalent to immortality. After many generations the senescent protozoa become very much shrunken and finally perish. People who enjoy—if enjoy is the word—a special longevity must also eventually die.

Is this the fate of the Jews, who have survived the Babylonians, the Persians, the Greeks, and the Romans? Will they also lose that identity which they have preserved so long a time? And in what way is the death or the disappearance of a senescent group different from that of an individual?

One can put these questions differently. In 1958 John F. Kennedy published a little book entitled *A Nation of Immigrants.* Will the Jews always be a nation of migrants? Will they always adhere to their ancient religion? Will they never have a country of their own, like other nations? Will they remain a nation or a religious group? While I do not pretend to be a prophet and cannot answer those questions, I do have a personal opinion. It was partly formed by the acceptance of the repetition-compulsion theory and by the interpretation of some signs that seem to anticipate what is yet to be.

This is the minority opinion of one, my tentative answer to these questions. The Jews will always form a special nation or quasi-national group as long as there is oppression or discrimination or as long as different nations or national groups exist as such, which I hope will not be too long. The majority of Jews will always unflinchingly and tenaciously adhere to their religion as long as there are religions. But there is a strong probability that we are becoming a godless society in which other agencies govern the conduct of individuals and groups.

The social function of the Jews has already been discussed. It was said that they cannot perish until they have fulfilled that function. Only then will they be absorbed into a society which does not acknowledge separate nations and states. Only after they have fulfilled their function of uniting peoples will they give up their identity. Until that time they cannot vanish. The reader is reminded of earlier remarks dealing with the achievement of groups and its connection with the groups' will to live.

But what of the repetition compulsion? It is a powerful compulsion dictated by an intense inner necessity. Yet it is not all-powerful; it is not omnipotent.[44] It will be slowly but surely overcome by other tendencies, especially by the power of Eros, by the love of mankind.

Is this idea of the future utopian? I do not believe that we in our time shall live to see that state of affairs, nor will our grandchildren—perhaps not even their grandchildren. But some day that situation will come to pass. We can only see it at a distance, but we can see it. The fact that a very distant place can be seen but vaguely does not prevent it from being real.

Only a few words remain to be said about the future attitude of the Jews and gentiles toward the solution. The fact that their past was different need not prevent them from building a common future together.

The splendid isolation of persons and groups can last a long time, but it is always penetrated finally—in the life of persons as well as in that of groups.

We never work things out alone, neither as persons nor as groups. We always need others—persons or groups.

Notes and References

NOTES TO PART ONE

1. *Erewhon,* chap. 14.
2. I refer here to books such as *The Bible as History* and *The Bible as History in Pictures,* by Dr. Werner Keller, translated by Dr. William Neil. New York, Morrow, 1956, 1964.
3. Compare the discussion of historicity of the patriarchs in my book *The Temptation,* New York, Braziller, 1961, especially pp. 45 ff.
4. *The Changing Pattern of Old Testament,* Howard H. Rowley, Allenson, London, 1959.
5. In *Le Discours sur la Méthod,* 1637.
6. New York, Atheneum, 1961, edited by Marie Bell.
7. Appeared first in *Imago,* 1915 Vol. I. Now in *Gesammelte Schriften.* Vol. X., 332 ff. First English translation in Freud, *War, Sex and Neurosis,* edited by Sandor Katz, New York, 1947.
8. Samuel Taylor Coleridge, *Biographica Literaria,* New York, Dutton, 1952. Vol. I. p. 442.
9. Arnold Toynbee deals with a similar subject in his paper "Conditions of Survival," *Saturday Review,* Aug. 29, 1940, and contrasts the self-centeredness of the individual with his superpersonal interests.

NOTES TO PART TWO

1. Farrar, Straus, New York, 1956, p. 647.
2. *Flaubert und Seine Versuchung des Heiligen Antonius, Ein Beitrag zur Kunstler Psychologie,* with a Preface by Alfred Kerr. Minden in Westfalen, 1912. As far as I know, the first psychoanalytic Ph.D. thesis in Europe.

3. *Our Attitude Towards Death,* in the standard edition of *The Complete Psychological Works of Sigmund Freud,* London, 1961, Vol. XIV, p. 298.

4. Quoted from the Modern Library Edition, Random House, New York, 1946, p. 139.

5. P. Dupré, *Encyclopédie des Citations,* Paris, 1959, p. 255.

6. Othon Guerlac, *Les Citations Françaises,* Paris, 1957, p. 325.

7. First part, sixth book, *De Remords et de la Conscience.*

8. Article in *Revue de Litteratures Comparées,* September, 1930, pp. 521-23.

9. Standard edition of *The Complete Psychological Works of Sigmund Freud,* Vol. XXI, p. 125.

10. Ernest Jones, *Life and Work of Sigmund Freud,* Vol. I, p. 20.

11. Ernest Jones, *op. cit.,* Vol. III, p. 245.

12. It gave me great satisfaction that Freud liked my short paper in this book. (Translated *From Thirty Years with Freud,* Rinehart, New York, 1940, p. 197). Freud wrote to me on April 16, 1930: "Thanks for your article on my *Civilization and Its Discontents.* It is the best and most dignified of all I have read about it until now." Quoted from *The Search Within,* Farrar, Straus, New York 1956, p. 649.

13. I take these and the following data from the third volume of the Ernest Jones biography in which the years 1919-1939 are dealt with.

14. Standard edition of *The Complete Psychological Works of Sigmund Freud,* Vol. XIX. p. 125.

15. The study on Dostoevsky was begun much earlier than 1928, but was put aside because Jolan Neufeld has written a book, *Dostoevsky: Sketch to his Psychoanalysis,* published in 1923 in Vienna, in which some of Freud's views are anticipated. Freud's study on Dostoevsky forms the introduction of the volume *Die Urgestalt der Brüder Karamasoff,* edited by Fritz Echstein and René Fülöp-Miller, in the German translation of Dostoevsky, 23 volumes.

16. My critical essay, as well as Freud's letters to me, appears in *From Thirty Years with Freud,* Rinehart, New York, 1940, pp. 155ff.

17. Later addition: one of those reasons that had remained unconscious for a long time was certainly by vanity. Freud wrote in that letter, "I have read your criticism of my Dostoevsky study with great pleasure. All your objections are worth considering and certain of them I admit have hit the nail on the head."

18. In *Revue de Litteratures Comparées,* July-September, 1930, No. 3, p. 520.

19. *Collected Papers*, ed. by Ernest Jones, Basic Books, New York, 1959, Vol. IV.
20. Scribner's, New York, 1962.
21. *Macbeth*, II, ii.
22. Ernest Jones, *The Life and Work of Sigmund Freud*, Vol. II, p. 266.
23. Freud, *Note Upon a Case of Obsessional Neurosis, Collected Papers*, Vol. III.
24. *Totem and Taboo*, Norton, New York, 1952. Originally published in Vienna, 1913.
25. *"Les gens que vous tuez se portent assez bien." Le Menteur*, 1643.
26. A reproduction of this photograph hangs now above my desk. To the lines about Freud's attitude to death, compare Jones, *op. cit.*, Vol. III, p. 152. Freud said it was a "terrifying thought" that his mother would hear of his death. When she died, aged ninety-five, Freud had, as Jones reports (p. 152) "a feeling of liberation, of release" which Freud understood in the following sense: "I was not allowed to die as long as she was alive, and now I may."

    Dr. Max Schur, who had been Freud's physician until the end, told us many things of interest in his Freud Memorial Lecture "The Problem of Death in Freud's Life and Theory," on May 19, 1964. For instance, Freud, in spite of his prolonged and terrible suffering, never considered suicide. Dr. Schur confirmed that Freud set himself "deadlines" and that the theory of life-and-death-instinct presented Freud's theoretical attempt to analyze his attitude to his own death.
27. Mentioned in my book *Myth and Guilt*, Braziller, New York, 1957, p. 10.
28. Ernest Jones, *op. cit.*, Vol. II, p. 354.
29. *Ibid.*, p. 350.
30. Compare also my book *Masochism in Modern Man*, Farrar, Straus, New York, 1949, and *The Compulsion to Confess*, Farrar, Straus, 1959.
31. *Myth and Guilt*.
32. Compare Robert N. Buller, in *Psychiatry*, February, 1963. Vol. 26, pp. 65ff.
33. "Über die Wirkung imbewurster Todeswunsche," *Internationale Zeitschrift fris ärztliche Psychoanalyse*, Vol. II, 1914.
34. Farrar, Straus, New York, 1949.
35. Freud shows in his *Civilization and Its Discontents* that it is not possible to conceal the continuing existence and the effects of forbidden wishes from the superego.
36. *A Letter to Myself*, Farrar, Straus, New York, 1964, p. 13.

37. E. W. Howe, *Country Town Sayings,* New York, 1911.
38. Now contained in *The Complete Psychological Works of Sigmund Freud,* Vol. XVII.
39. Page 53.
40. Compare Ernest Jones, *op. cit.,* Vol. I, p. 7, and Maria Bonaparte, Anna Freud, Ernest Kris. *Aus den Anfängen der Psychoanalyse,* London, 1930. For the literature on Goethe's childhood memory compare also J. Harnick, "Zum Hinauswerfen von Gegenständen aus dem Fenster durch Kleine Kinder," *Internationale Zeitschrift für Ärztliche Psychoanalyse,* VI, 1920, pp. 160-163.
41. *Sämtliche Werke,* Bettina Brentano, Berlin, 1920-22.
42. From an address entitled "The Personality and Career of Satan," *Journal of Social Issues,* 1962, Vol. XVIII.
43. *A Letter to Myself,* p. 234.
44. *The Psychoanalytic Theory of Neurosis,* Norton, New York, 1945, p. 217.
45. Baron Dirsztay is mentioned several times in Alma Mahler Werfels, *And the Bridge Is Love,* London, Hutchinson, 1959, p. 125. In Dirsztay's novel *Der Unintrinnbare* (with drawings by Oskar Kokoschka, Kurt Wolff Verlag, Munich, 1923), the figure of Gustav Mahler plays an important part. Dirsztay, who had once been a patient of mine, dedicated that novel "in gratitude" to me.
46. Farrar, Straus, New York, 1953.
47. For this part I used especially the following books: Bruno Walter, *Gustaf Mahler,* translated by Lotte Walter Lindt, Knopf, New York, 1958; Bruno Walter, *Theme and Variation,* an autobiography, translated by James A. Galston, Knopf, New York, 1946; and Mae Graf, *Bruno Walter and Gustav Mahler,* in *Oesterreichliche Musikzeitschrift,* Vienna, April, 1948.
48. Compare for details about the meeting of Freud and Mahler. Ernest Jones, *op. cit.,* Vol. II, and the letter Freud wrote to me about it published in my *The Haunting Melody,* p. 343.
49. This is Otto Fenichel's characterization in *The Psychoanalytic Theory of Neurosis,* p. 217.
50. Bruno Walter, *Gustav Mahler.* See pages 10, 31, 164.
51. *The Mold of Murder,* New York and London, 1961, pp. 40ff. This author often refers to my book *The Unknown Murderer* and calls it "a classical work"!
52. The widespread belief in the evil eye was discussed in the article of F. T. Eworthy in the Vol. V of *The Encyclopedia of Religion and Ethics,* Edinburgh, 1912. pp. 600 ff. There also is literature on the subject.
53. J. Bryon, "The Evil Eye," *Holiday,* May, 1964.

54. "The Ballad of Reading Gaol," 1898, part VII.
55. In *Archive of Neurology and Psychiatry*, 1959. Vol. 81. pp. 36off.
56. *Group Psychology and the Analysis of the Ego*, translated by James Strachey, London, Intern. Psychoanalytic Press, 1922.
57. Gustave Le Bon, *Psychologie des Foules*, Paris, 1895.
58. Benson Carmichael, "The Death wish in Daily Life," *Psychoanalytic Review*, 1943.
59. Dr. Hector Ripley, "A Psychiatrist's Evaluation on the Assassination of President Kennedy, *The Pastoral Counsellor*, Spring, 1964.
60. "On the Threshold of Despair," *New York Times*, April 5, 1964.
61. In Introduction to Psychoanalysis of War Neurosis, Intern. Psychoanalytic Press, London, 1931.
62. London Records with the Vienna Philharmonic Orchestra and the State Opera Chorus.
63. *Correspondence*, Open Letters, published by the Institute International de Cooperation Intellectuelle in Paris, Vol. II. "Why War?", 1933. The series was published simultaneously in German, English, and French.
64. Farrar, Straus, New York, 1948, p. 513.
65. *New York Times*, July 31, 1964.

NOTES TO PART THREE

1. "Remembering Jewish History," *Commentary*, February, 1964, p. 76.
2. Quoted from Franz Rosenzweig, *Der Stern der Erlösung*, Heidelberg, 1954, III, 199.
3. First published in German under the title *Jenseits des Lustprinzips*, Vienna and Leipzig, 1920. In English in 1922. Here quoted from the Standard Edition of *The Complete Psychological Works of Sigmund Freud*, London, 1955, Vol. XVIII, 13ff.
4. Especially in his book *Group Psychology and the Analysis of Ego*, New York, Liveright, 1922.
5. *Collected Papers*, Vol. IV.
6. Lawrence Kubie, "Critical Analysis of the Concept of a Repetition Compulsion," *International Journal of Psychoanalysis*, Vol. XX, 1939. Other contributions Imre Hermann, Randbemerkung en zum Wiederholungszwang, *Intern. Zeitschrift für Psychoanalyse*, Vol. 18, 1927. Edward Bibring, "The Conception of the Repetition Compulsion," *Intern. Psychoanalytic Quarterly*, 1943. Good examples of repetition compulsion are in Ludwig Jekel's paper, "Psychoanalysis and Dialectic," *The Psychoanalytic Review*, Vol. 28, No. 2, April, 1941.

7. In *The Jews, Their History, Culture and Religion,* edited by Louis Finkelstein, 3d Edition, New York, 1960, I, 3 ff.

9. *Ibid.,* p. 4. The most widely accepted theory that Arabia was the cradleland of the Semites can also point to the fact that the Arabic language has preserved a far larger proportion of primitive Semitic tongues. (George A. Barton in his articles on the "Semites," in *Encyclopedia of Religion and Ethics,* Vol. II, 379.)

9. "Josephus Contra Apionem," I, 22. This and the following data are taken from the excellent book *Judenfeinschaft,* edited by Karl T. A. Fischer, Frankfort-am-Main, 1963, especially pp. 7ff.

10. *Histories,* Vol. XIII, p. 91.

11. *Histories,* Vol. V, p. 13.

12. *Ibid.,* p. 5.

13. *Genèse de l'Antisemitisme,* Paris, 1956. I translated from the French, p. 77. Compare also James Parkes, *Antisemitism,* London, 1962, especially pp. 57ff.

14. Kent, 1952, p. 12.

15. *Ibid.,* p. 43.

16. Hannah Arendt, *Eichmann in Jerusalem,* Viking, New York, 1963. I prefer Moshe Pearlman's *The Capture and Trial of Adolf Eichmann,* Simon & Schuster, New York, 1963.

17. *The Wandering Jew,* London, 1881.

18. Yoseloff, New York, 1960.

19. Paris, 1929.

20. Article on Semites in *Encyclopedia of Religion and Ethics,* Scribner's, New York, 1951, Vol. II, p. 382.

21. Compare the paper on family solidarity in my book *Pagan Rites in Judaism,* Farrar, Straus, New York, 1964.

22. *Jacob's Dream,* translated by Ida B. Whym, Philadelphia, 1946.

23. *Start from Somewhere Else,* Doubleday, New York, 1955, p. 155.

24. *Civilization and Climate,* New York, 1924, pp. 387ff. Huntington deals also with the hypothesis that climate ranks with racial inheritance and cultural development as one of the three great factors in determining the conditions of civilization.

25. *The Struggle between Desert and Son,* Jerusalem, 1955.

26. Vienna and Zürich, *Psychoanalytischer Verlag,* 1923, p. 58.

27. Page 57.

28. See *Pagan Rites in Judaism.* 1964.

29. See my book *The Temptation,* Braziller, New York, 1961, pp. 185ff.

30. See my book *Myth and Guilt,* Braziller, New York, 1957.

31. *Jewish Wit,* Gamut Press, New York, 1963.

32. In a private letter to me, dated January 15, 1963.

33. *Beyond the Melting Pot*, Nathan Glazer and Daniel Patrick Moynihan, Cambridge, Mass., 1963, p. 144.
34. Arnold M. Rose, *Anti-Semitism's Root in City Hatred in Race Prejudice and Discrimination*, New York, 1951, states that the Jews are conceived as "symbols of urban life."
35. Only a few samples of the vast literature on the subject are mentioned here: Bonz Cohen, *The Agricultural Life of the Jews in Babylon;* J. O. R. N. S., Vol. 27, No. 1, 1938. Gabriel Davidson, *Jews in Agriculture*, Chicago, 1943; and Vladimir Grossman, *The Soil's Calling*, Montreal, 1938.
36. A good orientation in this subject is offered by *Judenfeindschaft*. Herausgegeben bei Karl Thieme, Fischer Bücherei, Frankfurt-am-Main, May, 1963. For the study of the more recent history of anti-Semitism, see James Parkes' *Antisemitism*, Quadrangle, New York, 1964.
37. *Zur Judenfrage* 1843. Compare the discussion of this paper in *Judenfeindschaft*, 1963, pp. 175ff.
38. In the magazine *Midstream*, March, 1963.
39. *One Destiny*, Putnam, New York, 1945, p. 37.
40. Nikolai Berdyaev, *Christianity and Anti-Semitism*, Kent, 1952, p. 36.
41. *Ibid.*
42. *Encounter*, January, 1964, p. 51.
43. Compare the interpretation of election in my book *The Need to Be Loved*, Farrar, Straus, New York, 1963, pp. 6off.
44. Compare the interesting recent paper "The Repetition Compulsion and Maturational Drive Representatives," by Theodore Lipin, *Intern. Journal of Psychoanalysis*, Vol. 44, Part 4, 1963, 389ff.